ASIAN
FURNITURE

ASIAN
FURNITURE

A DIRECTORY AND SOURCEBOOK

EDITED BY PETER MOSS

With 451 color illustrations

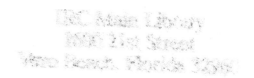

First published in the United Kingdom in 2007 by
Thames & Hudson Ltd, 181A High Holborn,
London WC1V 7QX

www.thamesandhudson.com

First published in 2007 in hardcover in the United States of America by
Thames & Hudson Inc., 500 Fifth Avenue, New York, New York 10110

thamesandhudsonusa.com

British Library Cataloguing-in-Publication Data
A catalogue record for this book is available from the British Library

Library of Congress Catalog Card Number: 2007901127

ISBN: 978-0-500-51378-1

Printed and bound in Hong Kong

CONTENTS

Furniture, the apparatus of domestic life, was intended for a sedentary role, not for travel. It is one of history's minor ironies, therefore, that furniture has led almost as peripatetic an existence as any other aspect of social dispersion. It has travelled far and wide, influenced whole cultures, cross-pollinated others and evolved unique geographical styles as a result of its exposure to outside influence.

For centuries the two terrestrial equivalents of oceanic currents kept the European and Asian worlds circulating in largely separate gyrations, only occasionally spilling across each other's outer peripheries through the voyages of Arab traders and penetrations by Mongol invaders. Furniture, tending not to be readily stowed on heavily laden dhows, or strapped across the saddles of nomadic horsemen, was generally left behind.

Not until the western world commenced its increasingly large-scale incursions into the east, from the fourteenth century onwards, did furniture figure in the accessories that went along for the ride. Europeans venturing into the Orient, to establish their colonial outposts, were reluctant to wholly abandon their habitats, furnishings and lifestyles, no matter how unsuited these might prove in hotter climates. So they took it all with them, including entire wardrobes of clothing that might have been comfortable in Lisbon, Madrid, London or Amsterdam, but were distinctly not so in tropical temperatures.

If the heavier items of furniture were less readily transportable, they found local craftsmen to imitate the general forms and dimensions, leaving them free to extemporise with the lesser particulars. Hence developed that glorious miscellany of hybrids that constitutes the gallimaufry of Asian furniture, to which this portfolio is humbly dedicated.

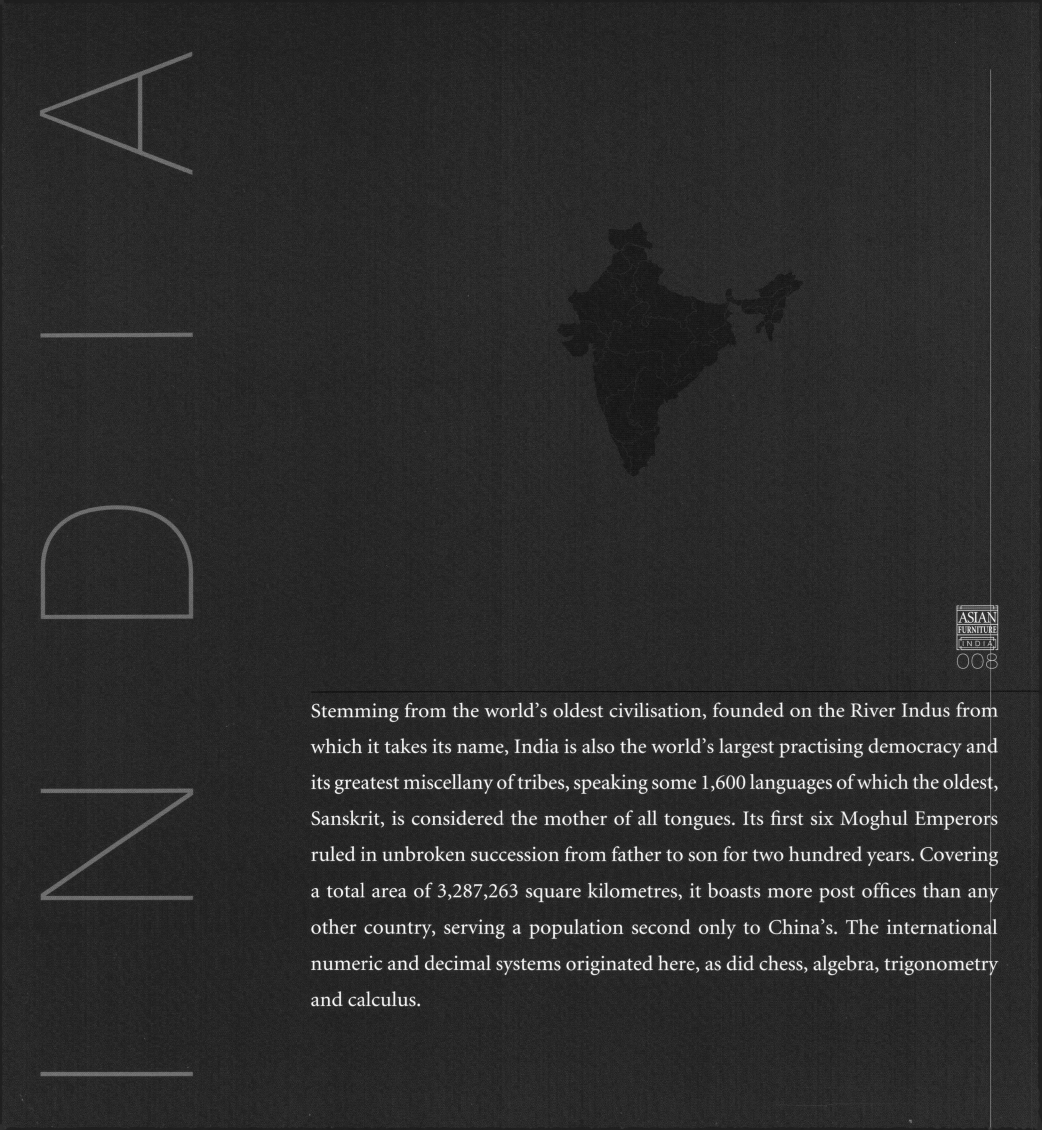

INDIA

Stemming from the world's oldest civilisation, founded on the River Indus from which it takes its name, India is also the world's largest practising democracy and its greatest miscellany of tribes, speaking some 1,600 languages of which the oldest, Sanskrit, is considered the mother of all tongues. Its first six Moghul Emperors ruled in unbroken succession from father to son for two hundred years. Covering a total area of 3,287,263 square kilometres, it boasts more post offices than any other country, serving a population second only to China's. The international numeric and decimal systems originated here, as did chess, algebra, trigonometry and calculus.

If Arabia had intrigued early European travellers with its unaccustomed manners and unfamiliar architecture, it had always been a strangeness hovering on their horizons and occasionally intruding, through incursions by marauding Asiatic tribes, into their geography.

India, on the other hand, positively threw open its doors to immerse them in exotica, provoking a sense of wonder perfectly captured by Van Dyck in the expression on the face of William Feilding, first Earl of Denbigh.

Indian craftsmen transformed chairs, tables, cabinets and sideboards into miniature marvels, often quite astonishing to behold.

Denbigh travelled to India in 1631–33, to visit the Mughal Court, and Van Dyck portrays him in a silken red and gold Hindu suit, apparently out hunting. By his side stands a young Indian servant, pointing to a parrot in the palm tree above.

The subject of the painting resembles a somnambulant walking wide-eyed through a dream. So overwhelmed is he, by all he has encountered, that he extends the fingers of his left hand in a gesture of renewed astonishment. Perhaps the brilliance of the parrot, or the extraordinary sounds it is making, have exceeded the bounds of his sensibilities.

He was fortunate to live in an age that held unlimited surprises, when the sheer varieties of landscapes and peoples, fauna and flora, art and architecture, fashions and furniture, could still thrill and enthrall the uninitiated.

India, in particular, was a vast storehouse of riches beyond the wildest expectations of its newest arrivals. Here the world's earliest known civilisation had developed in the Indus valley around 3000 BC. And following Alexander the Great, whose coming in 327 BC left Hellenic traces in its architecture, numerous other conquerors had contributed to its variegated cultural accretions before they in turn were conquered by India.

India was ever the great absorber, vanquishing its victors and adding them to its gallimaufry of trophies. Hence Britain, as its last coloniser, bequeathed to India a whole and distinct cultural legacy known as 'The Raj', which still rampantly survives in Indian lifestyles and fashions, manners and furniture, while in turn the British became so infected by India that today the popularly voted favourite meal on their menu is Indian curry.

But if Britain left behind more than it took away, the great Nabobs of the British East India Company – the engine that drove its empire – frequently returned home, towards the close of their relatively short lives, laden with more than wealth, honours and souvenirs. India left an ache in their memories from which they never fully recovered, so that they were disposed to bedeck their palatial but otherwise very English country estates with domes, minarets and other appurtenances of Indo-Saracenic architecture.

Into these homes went frequently spectacular assortments of furniture, though little or none of it would have been originally indigenous to India. For in all the bounty that India could offer its discoverers, furniture played an insignificant part.

Domestic furniture of the kind known in Europe was not traditional in India before the 16th century, and even such familiar objects as tables and chairs were rarely used until the successive arrivals of the Portuguese, Dutch, French and English. India's place in the world of furniture stems from its skilful adaptation and transformation of imported Western originals, to produce an independent Indo-European style of furniture much admired for its own sake, which subsequently exerted fresh influences in the West.

It was the boomerang effect, except that when the boomerang returned it was unexpectedly ornamented and elegantly wrought in ivory, bone, horn, silver and other exotic embellishments.

Previous page: Ornately embellished brass doors at the Rambagh Palace, Jaipur, open invitingly to visitors.
Opposite page: (Upper) The Gateway of India commemorates the visit of King George V and Queen Mary to Mumbai in December 1911.
(Lower left) Dating from 1857, the Indo-Saracenic façade of the University of Mumbai's historic Fort Campus epitomises the grandiose architectural precepts of its time. (Lower right) The Flora Fountain in the heart of the business district of Mumbai, built of Portland stone in 1864.

Extravagance of Indian Furniture

Peter Moss

What the Mongols were to China, the Moghuls were to India. They came, they saw, they conquered – and they stayed. The pattern was no accident, for *"Moghul"* was the Persian word for Mongol. Asia's two greatest dynasties sprang from the same heartlands in the treeless, horse-ridden plains at its continental core.

And as the Mongols had in China, the Moghuls too found that the longer they remained, the more inextricably entangled they became in their subjugated dominions – until India, in turn, conquered them.

Today the entire Indian panorama is conditioned by that exotic Moghul fibre interwoven into the fabric, its vistas framed in the arabesques of Indo-Saracenic ornamentation, its tapestries dominated by monumental Moghul architecture.

But the Moghuls were latecomers on the Indian scene. More than a century elapsed, following the death of China's greatest Mongol emperor, Kublai Khan, before his descendant, the far-ranging Timur the Lame, arrived on the banks of the Indus to commence his brief but ferocious Indian campaign. This led to the devastation of Delhi, not at Timur's command but simply because his hordes could not be reined back.

Another century would pass before Timur's heir, Babur, the true founder of India's Moghul dynasty, himself fell upon Delhi from the mountain passes of Afghanistan. Where Timur was named after the Uzbek word for iron, Babur gained his sobriquet from the Persian word for tiger.

Unlike his father Teragai, who retired to a Muslim monastery, telling his son "the world is a beautiful vase filled with scorpions", Timur resolved to shatter the vase and release the scorpions, leading them on paths of conquest that stretched from China to Turkey.

Though fired in the same forge, Babur's orientation leant more towards the western end of that sweeping arc his ancestor had slashed across central Asia. Where Timur was unmistakably Mongol in his provenance, Babur was Turkish in his leanings and his army was an eclectic ethnic mix of every strain from Anatolia to Samarkand.

He was amazingly fit, and legend has it that he made a point of swimming across every major river in India, just for the exercise. His hold on the country was nevertheless superficial, confined to its northern territories and terminated with his death in 1530, just three years after his arrival from Kabul. It was left to his grandson, the magnificent Akbar, to consolidate the Moghul hold on India.

Akbar was a born administrator, with the skills of a diplomat. In 1563 he abolished a tax levied on pilgrims to Hindu shrines, and the following year terminated the annual tax on unbelievers that had been imposed in return for Muslim protection. Under the pretence of hunting, he remained in constant motion around his extensive domains, attended by a large army and holding court in splendid encampments laid out like cities under canvas. While a great deal of hunting did occur, using trained cheetahs to pursue deer, the underlying purpose was political, displaying a show of strength, that fell short of open warfare, to negotiate treaties and marriages and generally keep informed of what was going on.

A man of whims, quirky, wilful and unfailingly original, Akbar moulded the Moghul style which, though often astonishingly intricate and ornate, at the same time embodied an indefinable sense of impermanence, as if its author might at any time lose patience with its consequence and embark on yet another hunting expedition.

It was Akbar who commissioned – and then abandoned in 1585, after a mere fourteen years – the jewelled marvel of Fatehpur Sikri, a hilltop citadel made up of courtyards and exotic free-standing buildings, constructed on a linear Hindu configuration instead of the gentler curves of Islam. Beams and lintels and even floorboards were cut and elaborately carved, much as if the material were oak rather than red sandstone.

Vaulted alabaster ceilings, onyx columns, graceful archways,
crystal chandeliers, and a dramatic cantilever stairway are hallmarks
of the Taj Mahal Hotel in Mumbai, which first opened its doors in 1903.

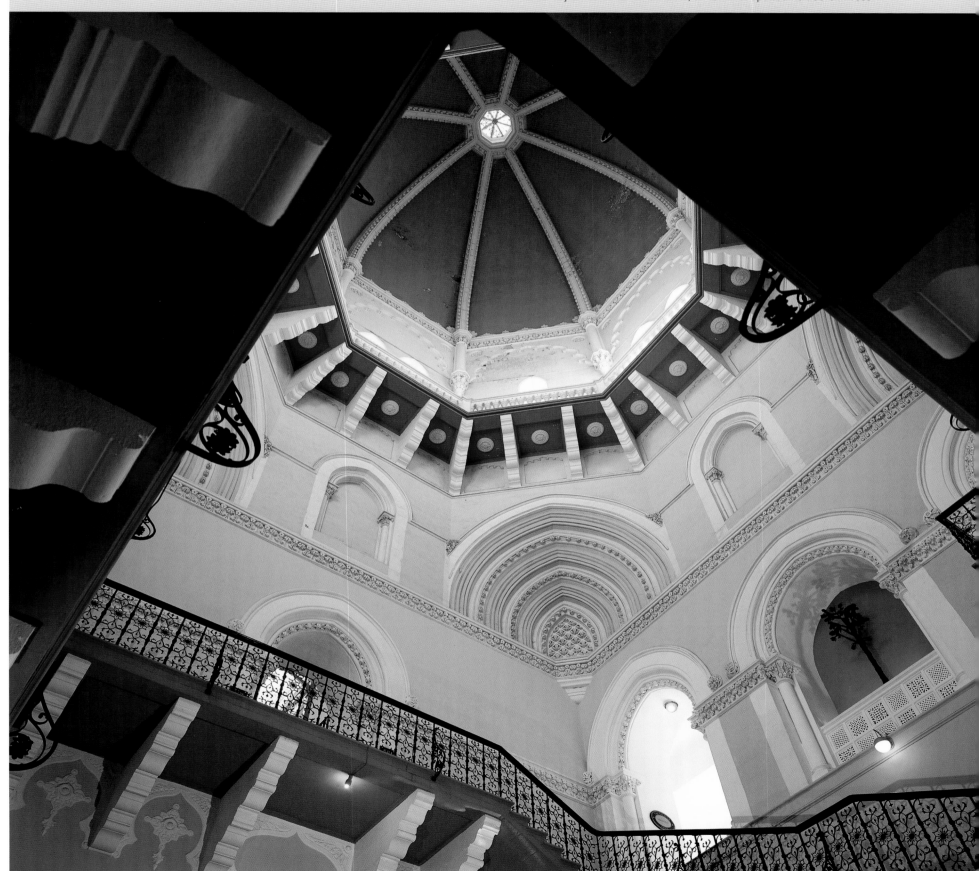

The Moghul Mode

Productive of extravagant architectural splendours, the Moghul mode placed scant emphasis on furniture, which was never really suited to the peripatetic existence of itinerant herdsmen turned nomad-warriors. Even the most potent of Moghul potentates chose to recline on carpets and cushions, elevated above lesser mortals on nothing more pretentious than a wooden dais, sometimes octagonal in shape.

Every home of any means was embellished with intricately carved wooden doors, windows, columns, brackets and panels. But while the country's mosques were magnificent, its temples ornate and its palaces ostentatious, they remained sparsely fitted out in anything like a western sense of what that phrase entailed.

Mahatma Gandhi seized upon western imagination with the simplicity of a spartan life furnished by little more than a spinning wheel, but he sprang from a long tradition that, aside from the structural grandeur of its religious shrines and princely courts, had eschewed bodily comfort in favour of spiritual enlightenment.

Above all, it was this asceticism that most astonished early western arrivals in that strangely different land. In his book *The Past in the Present: India as Museum of Mankind,* Bernard S. Cohn portrays India as it was first seen through western eyes, alternately a home of "gentle gymnosophists, ascetics and philosophers" or a realm of "threatening and bizarre marvels".

What they witnessed both fascinated and repelled these first arrivals on Indian shores; religious devotees practising various forms of physical penance in an attempt to transcend bodily and earthly desires, *fakirs* and *sadhus* enduring fanatical extremism which made them seem "more like devils than living men". The sole bodily comfort that the less rigorously self-mortifying of these peoples appeared to allow themselves was a *charpoy*, a light wooden bedstead strung with cord.

The British, when they finally subdued the last of the Moghuls, ousting the Dutch and the French in their determination to seize this jewel for their crown and leaving only the Portuguese undisturbed in their original settlement at Goa, decided that they were not going to descend to the basics of the native lifestyle. If the comforts of home were generally lacking, they would introduce their own.

Thus – through colonial intervention – furniture came to India, not ethnic, not indigenous but imported from Europe – and then transmogrified by Indian carpenters into forms vastly superior to the originals. Indian craftsmen, assigned to replicate these curious contrivances so dear to their colonial masters, decided to lavish upon them the same care and attention to detail that they reserved for their own temples and palaces. They transformed chairs, tables, cabinets and sideboards into miniature architectural marvels, heavily incised, deeply inlaid and often quite astonishing to behold.

Colonial Influence

Although the most tenacious, the British were not the first colonists to transport their goods and chattels into these new domains. As had the Spanish in the Philippines, the Portuguese, Dutch and French all imposed their own styles and tastes onto the emerging development of what we now know as Indian furniture.

The Indo-Portuguese influence produced a northern Indian, or provincial Moghul, style and a southern, or so-called Goanese, style. Artistically the more interesting, the former included a variety of furniture decorated with inlaid bone or ivory on ebony and other dark woods. Also found in this category were tables and writing cabinets in the Italian Renaissance form, which at that time was dominant in Portugal.

The second Indo-Portuguese style, sometimes called Goanese although in fact it more probably stemmed from the Malabar Coast, south of Goa, was more stereotyped in decoration, distinguished by large and cumbersome cabinets of a type known in Portugal as *contador*. The inlay ornamentation of these cabinets was either geometrical or semiabstract. Doubtless

The heritage wing of the Taj Mahal Hotel is an architectural marvel, bringing together Moorish, Oriental and Florentine styles.

this resulted from the fact that the South Indian contribution was more inhibited, lacking the charm and fancifulness of the northern Indo-Portuguese variety.

Easily distinguishable from Indo-Portuguese was Indo-Dutch furniture, since the latter reflected contemporary Dutch taste as clearly as the former reflected Portuguese. Of the two types of Indo-Dutch furniture, the first was made on the Coromandel Coast, chiefly of light-coloured woods decorated with inlaid bone, incised and lacquered. The second was a style of carved ebony furniture which, although commonly found in India and often thought to be Indian in origin, was in fact made at Batavia in Java, Holland's administrative headquarters in the East. The carved relief decoration of this ebony furniture was closely related to the flowering-tree style of contemporary Indo-Dutch embroidered bedspreads and hangings in which the tulip was a prominent motif.

With the growth of British power in India in the eighteenth century, all Indo-European furniture styles came increasingly under the influence of The Raj. And the leading propagators of the Raj style were not so much the British themselves as the native princes who took to it, orb, crown and sceptre.

The British never governed the whole of India directly. About one third of the subcontinent and a quarter of its people remained under the rule of Hindu rajahs and maharajahs and Muslim nizams and nawabs. By the early nineteenth century, these proud princes were all under the ultimate control of the country's latest conquerors, allowed to remain on their thrones only so long as their British overlords considered them satisfactory rulers.

The manner in which the British exercised control of India was not unlike the manner in which oil relates to water. They overlaid, they suppressed, they soothed the turbulence but they refrained from mingling. They kept themselves apart. They had come to India to trade and had found it necessary to wage a few wars in order to assert their right to do so. But the wars, instead of calming India, had stirred things up, which necessitated further intervention, further stabilisation, until somehow, almost before they realised it, the British found themselves occupiers of the whole subcontinent.

With this unsought transformation from a trading to a governing power, the entire rationale for the Raj changed. Instead of making profits, the new objective was to make

India a better place. Instead of businessmen, Britain sent out 'improvers' educated in Indian languages, zealous secular propagators of Victorian values and morality. In a valedictory speech delivered in Bombay, Viceroy George Nathaniel Curzon, who was regarded by his contemporaries as the archetypical 'Superior Person', faithfully reiterated this ideal:

"Remember that the Almighty has placed your hand on the greatest of His ploughs, in whose furrow the nations of the future are germinating and taking shape, to drive the blade a little forward in your time, and to feel that somewhere among these millions you have left a little justice or happiness or prosperity".

Also among those millions were the few towards whom the British found it expedient to adopt a less patronising attitude, recognising that if they were to retain the valuable services of the native nobility they must display towards them a certain geniality that exceeded their habitual condescension.

The Age of Opulence

Such patronage led to officially sanctioned indulgence of the grandiloquent tendencies endemic in Indian aristocracy. Like pampered opera divas, permanently on stage before an admiring audience, the ruling class felt it *noblesse oblige* to stage performances of extravagant opulence in order to outdo their rivals in bidding for the favours of the imperial elite.

They lived like Byzantine emperors who had somehow outlived Byzantium. In keeping with their own sumptuous personages and idiosyncrasies, their palaces, forts, armouries and vaults were showcases of beautiful treasures on permanent display. In modern times no other country but India has displayed so many fabulous collections of precious stones, magnificent carpets, priceless porcelains, ornaments and jewellery of purest jade, and intricate carvings of gold, silver and ivory.

Wealthiest of all was the Nizam of Hyderabad, who possessed one of the world's richest collections of silver and jade. It is doubtful he ever took a full inventory of the wealth accumulated in his many palaces, but he was meticulous and well informed

enough to add considerably to the fantastic fortune that his forebears had amassed.

Although the Crown placed a restraining hand on their shoulders after the Mutiny of 1857, India's nobility were still masters in their own houses and free to spend their fabulous wealth as they wished, well into the twentieth century. Some chose to develop their lands, educate their subjects and play the role of enlightened despots. Others took to the polo grounds and the lifestyle of the proverbial playboy.

One who found the time and means to pursue both options was the ninth Maharajah of Gwalior, Sir Madha Rao Sindhia. Well meriting his description as a 'jolly nice chap', he was proudly western in outlook and staunchly pro-British. Eager for Western-style progress, he made Gwalior one of the most advanced states in India, balancing the budget, encouraging local industries, building schools and hospitals and providing honest judges who sent their prisoners to model jails. He also had a passion for hunting tigers, even writing a book on the subject – *A Guide to Tiger Shooting* – which became prescribed reading for British dignitaries invited to join him on his hunting parties.

Sir Madha Rao was not alone in this proclivity. In gorgeously caparisoned howdahs atop elephants covered in tiger-proof regalia, fellow rulers would regally entertain colonial guests to picnic lunches while in pursuit of both the jungle's primary predator and its lesser game. They lived their lives in full Technicolor as if starring in some endless cinematic epic of pomp and circumstance, and indeed Hollywood fell in love with them, featuring them in such romances as *The Rains Came*, based on the novel by Louis Bromfield and later remade as *The Rains of Ranchipur*.

But if the Raj encouraged them in their excesses, the maharajahs and their kind repaid the compliment by adopting, in turn, the trappings of the Raj which extended, in particular, to their unprecedented furniture.

Whole suites were made in ivory, in the manner of Chippendale and Sheraton, not only for European buyers but also for Indian

The Taj Mahal Hotel was originally designed to open its arms to the sea, but the architectural plans were accidentally reversed, to create this gracious oasis of an inner courtyard.

rulers who increasingly favoured European styles. It was thus the English persuasion towards which most Indian furniture leaned, producing articles greatly sought after by collectors excited to discover familiar forms irradiated by Indian taste and fashioned from prized and unusual materials.

Although the techniques employed were Indian, the decoration was primarily designed to appeal to European consumers. The result was a curious hybrid, known as Anglo-Indian furniture, as far removed from native Indian vocabularies of ornamentation as the furniture itself was from Indian tradition. It was the Indian carpenter's equivalent of *chop suey*, the immigrant Chinese chef's concession to European palates. To this extent, Anglo-Indian furniture was as exotic to the eyes of the people who crafted it as it was to those who commissioned it.

The mother of all Anglo-Indian furniture was the *almirah*, a tall, wardrobe-like receptacle for clothing, personal possessions, office equipment, files and not infrequently foodstuffs. The typical office *almirah* was so commodious and accommodating that it became something of a catchword as a repository of secrets. A recent issue of the web-based newsletter *India Together*, discussing official ineptitude in failing to deal with reports of inadequate welfare services, remarked "One can safely presume that these reports are gathering dust on some politician's table or in some bureaucrat's *almirah*".

In the eighteenth and early nineteenth centuries there were recognised centres for the production of the differing styles of ornamentation, for *almirahs* as much as for other items of furniture – Vizagapatnam, Murshidabad and Travancore for ivory work, Patna for painted furniture and Bombay for micromosaic inlay. But these centres multiplied with the expansion of British influence across the sub-continent, through the spread of the railways and the greater accessibility of remoter regions.

Reaching a Wider Audience

From the 1850s onwards, exposure of Anglo-Indian furniture to a wider audience – largely through international expositions such as the Great Exhibition of 1851 in London's Crystal Palace – resulted in a surge of interest even among those who had never been, or had no intention of going, to India. The India Court at the Great Exhibition displayed a range of Anglo-Indian furniture that included Bombay blackwood chairs and sofas, painted chests from Bareilly, boxes from Calcutta, Bombay and Vizagapatnam, a silver-covered bedstead from Benares, ivory chairs from Vizagapatnam and an ivory-veneered throne chair commissioned by the Maharaja of Travancore as a present for Queen Victoria.

Added to the earlier splendours of the Prince Regent's Brighton Pavilion, with its Moorish architecture, Oriental furnishings and astonishing collection of Chinoiserie, the Crystal Palace ensured that the authentic East had arrived in England in edifices large enough to be experienced as monumental architecture.

One reason why Anglo-Indian furniture was greatly admired by the Victorian public lay in the fact that the traditional craft skills which went into their manufacture were being replaced in Britain by machine-made goods. The insidious industrial revolution was not only shifting the country's power base northward, to the mills and factories of Birmingham, Manchester and Sheffield, but was eroding the market for hand-crafted wares.

Underpaid Indian carpenters, toiling with their lathes and chisels in foetid Bombay workshops, would have been bemused to hear European art critics arguing that the form, colour and ornamentation of Indian manufactures followed correct principles of design, whereas mass-produced goods from Britain did not.

Typical of the admiration accorded to Indian art manufactures of the later nineteenth century were the comments of Sir George Birdwood, a leading authority on their forms and provenance. Sir George remarked "In India everything, as yet at least, is hand-wrought, and everything, down to the cheapest toys and earthen vessels, is therefore more or less a work of art".

But everything Indian was already becoming rather "less a work of art" than Sir George envisaged. The market for Anglo-Indian furniture was outpacing the talent pool dedicated to its production. In his historical essay on Indian furniture, Joseph T. Butler records that during the nineteenth century Indian artistic standards degenerated, as was clearly reflected in the furniture of the period. The emphasis was on decorative elaboration for its own sake and, although much nineteenth-century Indian woodcarving showed great technical skill, this rarely compensated for formlessness and stereotyped ornament.

Birth of the Art Schools

The mid-nineteenth century had also witnessed the birth in India of art schools based on western models. It was felt that, skilled as they were, Indian craftsmen would benefit from western art education. Thus, through their inability to refrain from tampering, did the well-meaning and kindly Victorians unconsciously set out to kill, by degrees, the thing they loved. It was effectively the beginning of the end.

The art schools aimed at "preserving traditional craft skills in the face of declining patronage". In many cases this was achieved by encouraging Indian artisans to produce western-style goods that would find a ready market among the local European population. That this involved applying Indian ornamentation to western-style objects did not seem incongruous at the time. The hybrid tradition had been long established.

For the Empire of India Exhibition, held in London in 1895, Indian carpenters produced western-style furniture decorated "in purely Hindu style, the designs being taken from the temples of Madura, Vellore and Tanjore". At the Madras School of Art, furniture was based on designs of contemporary European cabinetmakers, their ornamental details adapted from Dravidian models.

At the other extreme, craftsmen were being instructed to make furniture completely divorced from any Indian aesthetic. One example was a commission by Mr. J. Gordon, who in 1864 instructed Punjabi inlayers to produce a specimen wood table inlaid with British heraldic shields.

For the Calcutta International Exhibition of 1882–83, a certain Mr. Whiteside supervised Madras carpenters as they laboured over historical revival furniture, including an Elizabethan sideboard copied from a drawing of the original at Cornishead Priory, Lincolnshire, a fourteenth century credence table and a "bedstead of ancient Byzantine pattern".

By the end of the nineteenth century some critics were beginning to recognise that, where Anglo-Indian furniture was concerned, things were getting a little out of hand. They were waking up to the absurdity of a sideboard carved in the style of an Ahmadabad mosque, or a chair decorated with scenes from the Ramayana.

By now too Indian royalty was losing interest in these home-made miscegenations and beginning to withdraw its patronage in favour of imported goods from Europe, which they regarded as far more powerful status symbols. Writing in 1912, Alfred Chatterton explained this phenomenon:

"The picturesque pageantry of the native courts has disappeared, and the descendants of the old chieftains and princes adorn their reception rooms with gilt mirrors, glass chandeliers and Parisian ormolu and bronzes. Musical boxes, mechanical toys and photographs excite their wonder and amuse their idle hours. The gilt and tinsel of European civilisation attract them and they no longer appreciate the artistic productions of their country. In consequence, the hereditary art workers have fallen upon evil days; to earn a livelihood they are forced to meet the demands of the dealers and cold-weather travellers for cheap imitations of what they were formerly encouraged to produce".

The tourist trade became the last resort of these beleaguered artisans. The old values slipped as they surrendered to the demand for instant souvenirs. What they had brought to the golden age of Anglo-Indian furniture in the nineteenth century was now but a memory.

Rationalisation of ornament, and overall simplification of early twentieth century Indian furniture, finally abolished the last remnants of demand for those flamboyant hybrid pieces produced at the zenith of their art. Where such furniture continued to be produced by the dedicated few, it was derided by the self-appointed cognoscenti, who determined that, as furniture was fundamentally western in both form and function, it was best decorated in a western manner.

The *Grammar of Ornament*

In his *Grammar of Ornament*, published in London in 1856, Owen Jones decreed that "Imitations, such as the graining of woods, and of the various coloured marbles, are allowable only when the employment of the thing imitated would not

have been inconsistent". Since his *Grammar of Ornament* was regarded by his arts contemporaries as the Bible of their times, Jones' "propositions" carried much weight.

His proposition 37 prophesised that "No improvement can take place in the art of the present generation until all classes, artists, manufacturers, and the public, are better educated in art, and the existence of general principles is more fully recognized". It is a proposition that holds as true today as it did then, for perhaps there never will be a perfect world where all classes are better educated in art.

It is possible that taste, like beauty, will forever lie in the eye of the beholder. That generalised eye was greatly smitten by what it beheld in Anglo-Indian furniture of the Victorian epoch, but the vision dimmed as the century progressed, and eventually died when the tide of empire receded, leaving its crossbred cultural fusions decaying on deserted strands.

It was perhaps a fitting end, in keeping with Patrick Conner's reminder, in his biography of the artist George Chinnery, that "As a species, the colonial expatriate has been likened to a deep-sea fish, whose constitution has been adapted to withstand high pressures in its normal existence near the sea bed – but which, when brought up to the surface, becomes swollen and distorted".

Conner postulates that it was not only the new environment which caused the colonial, like the deep-sea fish, to behave in an extreme and abnormal fashion; it was also his or her internal attributes that created this susceptibility to unaccustomed pressures. According to this theory, certain types of personality were attracted by the prospect of a colonial life, and once they achieved it they adopted the same excessive behaviour patterns as their predecessors in the colonial role.

When the high seas of colonial opulence ebbed below the horizon, all that greatly inflated excess was left floundering in the shallows, along with the other detritus – and the furnishings – of history.

सामान

Teak armchair with hard seat, openwork back splat of brass and ivory inlay. The front turned legs end in 'garlic-head' feet.

Armchair of eccentric design made of teak wood. Armrests terminate in lion head motif, the back splat is decorated with an inlay of the peacock – the national bird of India.

Square table with one drawer and matching chair of teak wood. Tabletop and apron delicately inlaid with ivory rangoli design – traditional rice patterns that offer praise to the Gods. Table and chair legs end in 'garlic-head' feet.

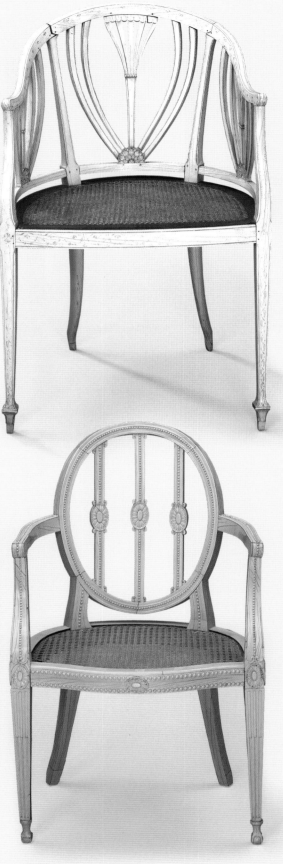

Armchair and footstool of solid ivory: turned, carved, pierced and partly gilt, with cane rosewood drop-in seat. The sides and backs are open. The footstool is upholstered in pink silk. Murshidabad. Bengal State. Early 19th century.

Armchair with continuing curved back of ivory. Upholstered seat. Gilt, openwork backrest and perpendicular front legs with splayed back legs. Murshidabad. Bengal State. Early 19th century.

Armchair with concave oval backrest with three vertical slats, each enhanced with rosette pattern. Wood veneered with ivory and contemporary upholstered seat. Front legs perpendicular, back legs splayed. Murshidabad. Bengal State. Late 18th century.

 Nawab (Muslim ruling prince), armchair and footstool of solid ivory. Backrest is pierced and partly gilt. Cane rosewood drop-in seats. The ivory footstool turned and partly gilt. Murshidabad. Bengal State. Early 19th century.

 Travelling armchair with rattan seat and circular footstool. Teak wood covered with sheet silver and enamel. The open backrest is supported by a top rail and connecting stretcher between the extended back legs. Lucknow. Uttar Pradesh. Circa 1820.

 An ornate pair of five-legged armchairs, sumptuously inlaid with engraved ivory, carved and gilt, with soft drop-in cane seats. The open back and sides each feature a splat decorated with pierced intertwining palm fronds and flowers. Murshidabad. Bengal State. Circa 1785.

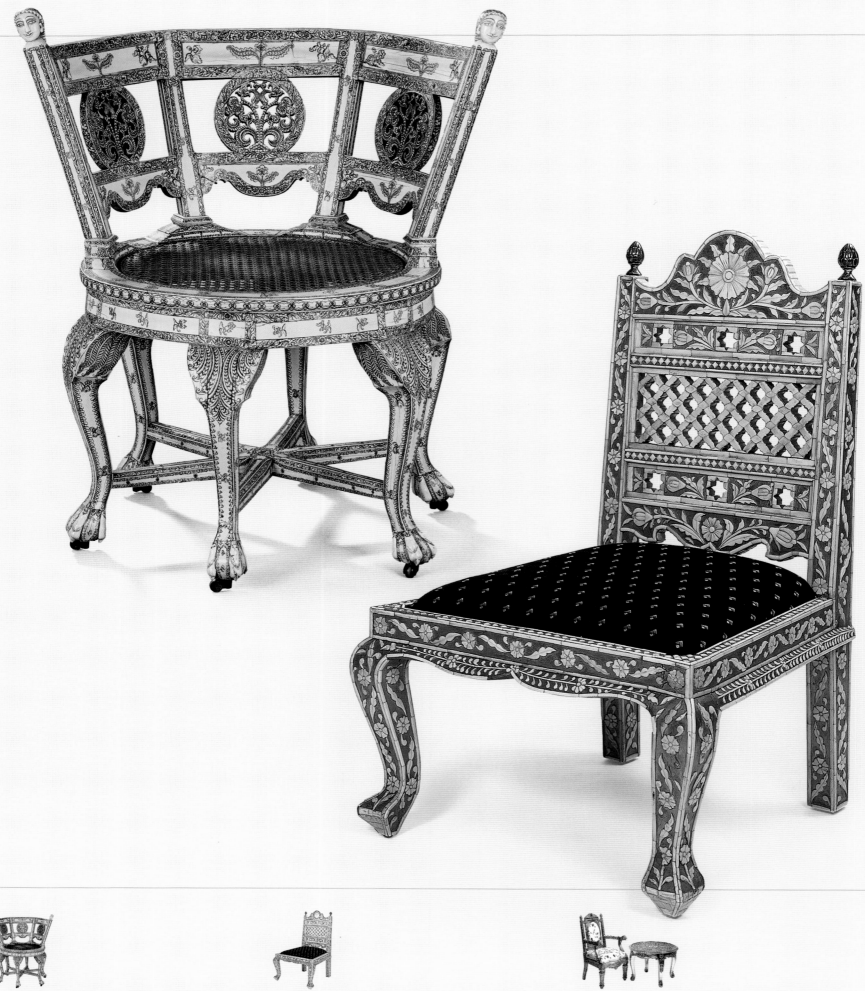

Six-legged circular armchair with curved backrest and woven rattan drop-in seat. Legs mounted on wheels are connected by six stretchers. Wood veneered with ivory. Vizagapatnam. Andhra Pradesh. Circa 1770.

Handcrafted chair of Burmese teak, overlaid with sterling silver. Openwork pierced decorative panel between back legs. Front legs curved. Seat of Noorjahan brocade ornately decorated with floral motif. Lucknow. Uttar Pradesh. Circa 1800.

Chair and circular table of Moghul design. Indian teak wood overlaid with sterling silver. Seat and backrest of Noorjahan brocade embroidery on jacquard. The surface of the matching four-legged table is embossed with a grapevine design.

Daybed of ebony carved and inlaid with ivory. The backrest and seat upholstered with crimson velvet. Only the front apron is carved, the rear is unadorned. Six legs connected by decorated stretcher. Vizagapatnam. Andhra Pradesh. Late 19th century. Light furniture with marquetry and inlay decoration were likely brought to Vizagapatnam by European traders in the early 18th century, and could have provided inspiration for the first inlaid furniture made there.

ANDHRA PRADESH

In 236 BC Satavahana established a kingdom around modern-day Hyderabad. Buddhism flourished in the kingdom though the rulers were followers of Brahmanism and it was during this period that the faith spread to China and the Far East. Aurangazeb, last Moghul king to rule India, conquered the Andhra in 1687 and left his governors to rule. The French and British succeeded them until India's independence. Andhra Pradesh retains much of its regal glory and charm.

 Love seat of sterling silver, with floral brocade embroidered with peacock motif. Backrest, arms and apron elaborately embossed. Legs terminate in ball and claw feet. Vizagapatnam. Andhra Pradesh. Circa 1770.

 Throne chair with upholstered seat and backrest and matching four-legged footstool. Handcrafted of Burmese teak. Overlaid with sterling silver. Back of the chair is embossed in silver, with motif of the dancing peacock, the national bird of India. Vizagapatnam. Andhra Pradesh. Late 18th century.

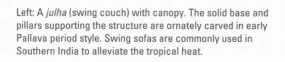 Left: A *julha* (swing couch) with canopy. The solid base and pillars supporting the structure are ornately carved in early Pallava period style. Swing sofas are commonly used in Southern India to alleviate the tropical heat.

 Chest with lacquered top and ornately carved front façade from State of Rajasthan. Painting shows Lord Krishna, who is always depicted in blue and surrounded by a gathering of admiring women.

 A stylised peacock of Indian teak. The Indian peacock is the symbol of personal pride and vehicle to Lord Murgan, the second son of Lord Shiva. The bird is especially revered when it struts, displaying its tail feathers in full regalia. In a formal dance to welcome the monsoon rains it spreads its fan of feathers, the eye on each said to ward off inauspicious spirits.

 An Indian palanquin (*palkis*) decorated in Rajasthan folk art motifs. Used by women and the elderly on social excursions, this type of sedan chair was carried by two porters.

Wedding palanquin. By tradition an Indian bride is escorted to the
groom's home concealed in an upholstered and curtained palanquin,
as custom demands that no one but the groom should set eyes on a bride
on her wedding day. Vizagapatnam. Andhra Pradesh. Late 18th century.

MADHYA PRADESH

The recorded history of Madhya Pradesh dates back to the time of Ashoka, the great Buddhist emperor. Between 950 and 1050 AD a fantastic series of temples was built at Khajuraho in the north of the state. From the 12th to the 16th centuries the region was the scene of continuous religious struggles between invaders. The Moghuls ultimately overcame local resistance, before succumbing to the Marathas, who in turn entered into treaties with the British in the 18th century.

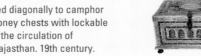

Shroff's (Accountant's) Cash Coffer. Brass splats affixed diagonally to camphor wood chest and arched lid, with pronounced rivets. Money chests with lockable lids were associated with finance houses dealing with the circulation of currency or the safekeeping of documents. Pushkar. Rajasthan. 19th century.

Shroff's (Accountant's) Cash Box. Rectangular chest elaborately ornamented with gold and black lacquer, embossed with brass plating. A lock secures the half-lid, which opens upward. Made of camphor wood. Sri Lanka. 18th century.

BENGAL

During the Mahabharatha period this area was divided into small kingdoms. Owing to its location, the region was a centre of trade with Cambodia, Burma, Sri Lanka, and the Persian Gulf. Calcutta remained the capital, until that honour was transferred to Delhi in 1912. When India gained its independence in 1947, Bengal was partitioned between India and Pakistan.

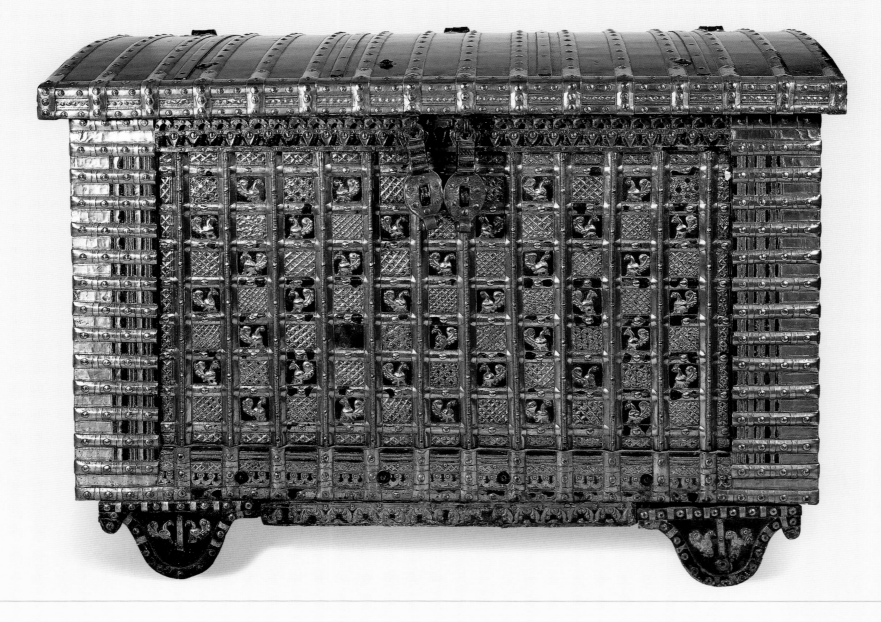

Safe Box. Desktop rectangular chest of camphor wood with handles, elaborately ornamented with gold and brass plating. Displayed with wooden elephant figure on rocking slats. Sri Lanka. 18th century.

Safe trunk or dowry (*damachia*) chest on wheels. Brass plated and embossed with peacock motifs. Before the development of a legal banking system, the Indian aristocracy used such chests made of camphor wood for the safekeeping of copper, gold and silver coins and documents of value. South India. Late 18th century.

 Waist-high rosewood cupboard, with five drawers and brass handle plates. Front façade intricately carved with flower motifs. North India. Contemporary.

 Low blackwood chest with three drawers. Decorated with open metal work. The lid opens upwards. Displayed is an ornate copper jug and salver used for the ritual washing of hands before prayers. Rajasthan. Contemporary.

Cabinet of ebony with three compartments. Fine filigree brass work decorates the front façade. On display is a peacock-shaped copper oil lamp. Maharashtra State. Contemporary.

Two-door cabinet of veneered wood with ivory. Made in Vizagapatnam. The city, originally the centre of textile production, has the only natural harbour between Madras and Calcutta on the Bay of Bengal. This combination attracted foreign traders, who introduced a demand for western-style furniture since the timber and ivory required were readily available from nearby forests. Late 18th century.

RAJASTHAN

Rajasthan, in India's northwestern corner, was invaded by waves of Afghans, Turks, Persians and Moghuls who integrated with the existing inhabitants and gave the Rajputs their martial heritage. The Moghul Emperor, Akbar, was the first to unite Rajasthan. In 1817 the British Government concluded treaties with Rajasthan and ruled it until Indian independence in 1947. Rajasthan's kingdoms left a rich architectural and cultural heritage, seen today in countless forts and palaces.

Small two-door vanity chest with four drawers. The insides of the doors are carved with mythical images of Adam and Eve standing either side of a tree, an indication that cupboards of this nature were destined for Western consumption. Sri Lanka. Late 17th century.

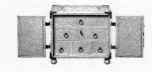

Small vanity chest of veneered wood and ivory. Two doors reveal six drawers with sterling silver drawer-pullers. The entire ivory surface of the cabinet is delicately carved in a rangoli pattern, also employed to decorate household entrances during Hindu festivals. Sri Lanka. Late 17th century.

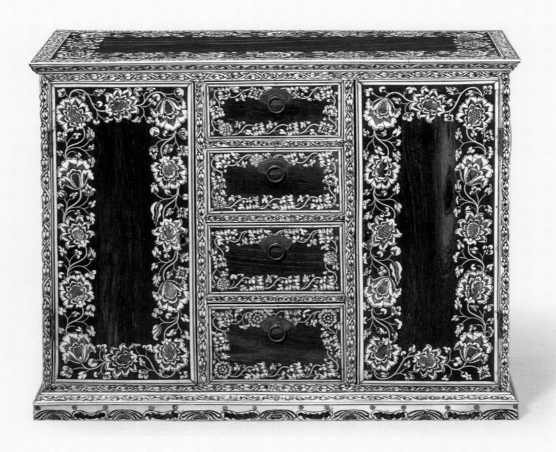

Four-drawer cabinet, wood inlaid with ivory. The decorative motif is floral. Both upper and lower apron are elaborately carved. Little is known about wood and ivory work at Vizagapatnam before the arrival of the Europeans in the mid 17th century, though the practice of embossing ivory on furniture for royal consumption existed in coastal Orissa. Vizagapatnam. Andhra Pradesh. Mid 18th century.

Royal wedding palanquin with oil lamps, overlaid with ivory fretwork. By Indian tradition a bride is escorted to the groom's home concealed in an upholstered and curtained palanquin, since custom demands that no one but the groom should set eyes on a bride on her wedding day. Vizagapatnam. Andhra Pradesh. Late 18th century.

Treasure box. Camphor wood veneered with pierced ivory. The box has carrying handles and two lockable drawers. The arched lid is also secured by a lock. The ivory motif is that of the Sri Lankan Gold Lion with sword of the Sinhalese kingdom of Kandy, when Sri Lanka was known as Ceylon prior to 1815.

Anglo-Indian Ivory Dressing Mirror.
Taking its design from Chinese export
lacquer pieces, it has five stepped tiers of
silver-handled drawers, each decorated
with a foliate scroll featuring a neo-classical
vase at the centre. The central oval mirror,
which retains it original plate, is surmounted
by a stylised ribbon and is supported by
serpentine shaped columns. Vizagapatnam.
Andhra Pradesh. 18th century.

 Cabinet of rosewood and ivory inlay with capital in the Empire-style, on a stand of four carbide formed legs. Upper cabinet has three drawers with sterling silver handles and a central door. Vizagapatnam. Andhra Pradesh. Late 18th century.

 Teapoy. From the Hindi *tinpai* (literally three legged or tripod). A refined tea table of classic shape; solid ivory, turned, carved and partly gilt. The circular top with gilt borders consists of three pieces of ivory and has a raised moulded rim. Murshidabad. West Bengal. 18th century.

 Games Table. Teak, partly carved, veneered with ivory, engraved and highlighted with red and black lacquer. The tabletop is configured for four-sided chess games, the squares and the board defined by borders of red and black crosses. The position of the nawah and wazir (king and queen), the four central squares for chequers and the corners of the board are engraved with lotus images. Travandrum. South India. 18th century.

The ornately decorated wooden balcony entrance to a Punjab home demonstrates the owner's status and offers a formal welcome to visitors and guests. Design elements show Moghul influences. Teak wood, 19th century.

INDONESIA

An archipelago of superlatives, Indonesia is the world's most extensive and scattered island chain, straddling two hemispheres and some 5,100 kilometres from west to east. Its 17,000 and more islands, comprising a total land area of some two million square kilometres, support a population of more than 200 million, living amid 400 volcanoes, of which at least 70 are still active. Both its ethnic mix and its history have proved as volatile as its geography, giving rise to successive waves of religions that have engulfed and obliterated earlier influences like strata laid down by consecutive eruptions.

This archipelago was once the world's most distant and sought-after,
coveted for its spices, its aromatic timbers and the exotica of a previously unknown culture.
Its astonishingly versatile bamboo was used for almost everything, from housing
to furnishing, from shipbuilding to daily utensils.

The earliest recorded alien incursions into the miscellany of islands now known as Indonesia can be traced to an influx of traders from Gujarat in Southeast India. In the course of the first century AD these were so well established that Indian scholars were reporting the existence of a Hindu kingdom known as "Dvipantara" or "Jawa Dwipa" in Java and Sumatra.

Within the same period Prince Aji Saka introduced writing into Java, based on scripts originating in southern India, and Hindu kings were ruling the area around Kutai in east Kalimantan, on the island of Borneo.

The archaic civilisations of Java and Sumatra were heavily influenced by India, initially through Hinduism and later through Buddhism, which peacefully coexisted with its predecessor, so that the archipelago's multifarious cultures, and even the one common language, still bear their traces.

This residue was never entirely erased, despite the subsequent arrival, in the 13th century, of Islam, whose more fanatical converts set out to efface all evidence of earlier creeds. Ironically the new Islamic influence was borne on the same currents that, centuries earlier, had carried Hinduism and Buddhism to these shores. This doctrine too was implanted by traders from Gujarat, who had themselves been converted through their trade contacts with Persia and the Middle East.

Islam undermined and eventually destroyed the great Majapahit empire that had ruled Java and much of the archipelago for more than two centuries, so powerfully that theirs, along with Japan, had been one of the few countries to defeat a Mongol invasion.

Descendants of the Majapahit aristocracy, religious scholars and members of the Hindu hierarchy, retreated through the East Java peninsula of Blambangan to the islands of Bali and Lombok. Bali was to remain staunchly Hindu while, in later years, eastern Lombok was converted to Islam, which entered the island from the southern Sulawesi city of Makassar, now named Ujungpandang.

Through all these centuries of ruling principalities, Hindu, Buddhist and eventually Muslim, the distinction between rulers and subjects was marked by a proliferation of artifacts on the one hand, and their marked absence on the other. Sumptuously appointed court protocols found their antithesis in the rustic simplicity of village life. However neither form was furnished in the sense that a westerner would understand.

As with other eastern codes of conduct, custom dictated that commoners should not stand taller than a king so that, if seated, the latter had to be elevated to a level that raised him above the multitude. But both would be sitting cross-legged, the one on a dais and the rest on the floor, for the concept of a chair was not introduced until the first Europeans arrived in 1509 with the advent of the Portuguese.

Close on the heels of the Portuguese came the Dutch, who retained their hold on the islands despite a brief interregnum by the British, based at Bengkulu in Sumatra from 1814 to 1826 under the indefatigable coloniser, botanist, anthropologist and explorer Sir Stamford Raffles. Aside from abolishing slavery and reforming the hated agricultural laws, under which crops were grown and surrendered to the Dutch, Raffles found time to write a remarkably comprehensive "History of Java".

It was principally the Dutch colonial style, however, that would leave its stamp on Indonesian furniture, and Indonesian craftsmen who would embellish the originals to produce a new and distinctive art form.

Previous page: Appropriately garbed in distinctive palace attire, a seated sentry guards the Kraton, an ancient palatial residence erected in Jogjakarta, central Java, in 1756.
Opposite page: (Upper) An island pavilion is the setting for a gamelan orchestra in the gardens of a Jakarta residence. (Lower left) The 10th century, earthquake-prone Prambanan Hindu temple complex, of central Java, is the largest of its kind in Indonesia. (Lower right) Stone relief on the crumbling façade of the temple complex.

Archipelago of Spices and Aromatic Woods:
Furniture of Indonesia

Soedarmadji J H Damais

Indonesia is a vast island-state covering most of the Malay archipelago in South-east Asia between the Indian ocean in the west, the Pacific ocean in the east and, in the middle, the South China and Java seas.

This archipelago comprises the islands of Sumatra, Kalimantan (Borneo), Sulawesi (the Celebes), Bali and the lesser Sunda islands, Maluku (the Moluccas) and Papua (the western part of New Guinea).

It is a very wealthy land with extensive jungles on islands like Kalimantan and Sumatra and intensively cultivated agricultural lands on others like Java and Bali.

This is the country which for centuries was known to the rest of the world for producing spices and rare woods. These woods, bamboo groves and other reeds were used for almost everything from housing to furnishing, from shipbuilding to daily utensils.

Fragrant woods like sandalwood (kayu cendana) and gaharu were exported to China and made into joss-sticks and small objects such as fans, boxes and statues.

Because Indonesians originally had no need of furniture for their homes, teak was used mainly for buildings and ships. One of the reasons the Dutch chose Java for their base in the archipelago was because of its vast teak estates. So furniture like chairs, chests, tables and cupboards were an introduction initially from India and later from China and Europe.

Armchairs or thrones were reserved for the élite in the community. Stone slabs and, later, massive wooden slabs were their predecessors. The backrest was a later development, to enhance the status of the occupant, and the wood used for this bore simple decoration and finish expressing the respective tribal cultures of the archipelago.

What the Chinese call *huanghuali* wood, used for furniture during the Ming Dynasty, is native to South-east Asia. Some other precious woods such as Sappan wood, Amboyna wood (Kayu Ambon), Macassar Ebony (kayu Sana Kling) etc., were found on Java and the neighbouring islands and were mostly exported for cabinet making.

All these types of wood have been used for centuries all over the world. Witness, in the recent past, the furniture designed by Parisian cabinetmaker Ruhlman in the 20s, employing a variety of these exotic woods from Indonesia like Ebene de Macassar (Macassar Ebony), Loupe d'Amboine (Amboyna Burr) and Bois de Palme (Coconut wood). We should be reminded that in the 17th century the term "Ebene" gave rise to "Ebeniste", the French word for a cabinetmaker.

Against this background, our overview of the history of furniture in Indonesia focuses primarily on the 18th and 19th centuries in discussing both European and Javanese productions found in public and private collections on the island of Java, for the majority of the furniture illustrated in the portfolio is drawn from this period.

Scrollback, covered writing desk common to offices managing coffee and sugar plantations. Teak wood. Late 19th century.

The Hindu Javanese kingdoms (7th–16th century)

Mataram (8th–10th century)

One of the earliest kingdoms of Java, Mataram produced the two vast temple complexes of Borobudur and Prambanan in Central Java. Through observing the bas-reliefs of these temples, which depict in stone the stories respectively of the Buddha and of the Ramayana, one can discover domestic scenes that reveal how people lived in Java in those days. The palaces are usually open pavilions with elaborate decorations very much like those that can still be seen in the Javanese 'kraton' and Balinese 'puri' palaces. The houses were ample wooden structures covered with thatch, as still seen in the tribal houses of Sumatra and Kalimantan.

Furniture was almost non-existent because people were seated on simple wooden platforms or on matting on floors. One can distinguish that royal couples lounged on sumptuous cushions while ascetics occupied rattan mats and only the Gods were seated on thrones. Here and there a profusion of baskets, pots and presentation plates on stands (dulang) fill the remaining habitable spaces of these scenes.

The concept of a throne seems to have been imported from South Asia either from Bengal, Sri Lanka or southern India, as is the term for it in both old and modern Javanese.

Majapahit (14th–16th century)

According to Odorico of Pordenone, an Italian Franciscan friar from the Veneto who visited Java in the 14th century, the King of Java had a large and sumptuous palace. Odorico must have visited Majapahit the capital of the east Javanese kingdom of the same name at the height of its power. Its cultural influence covered the entire Indonesian archipelago and even further on mainland South-east Asia.

The capital consisted of buildings with wooden pavilions standing on brickwork bases, very much the same as can be seen in Bali nowadays. Odorico says the King's palace was on stilts and the upper floors could be ascended by steps covered with alternating gold and silver leaf. The interior walls were decorated with sculpted wood panelling also covered with presumably 'prada' gold leaf. But he makes no mention of the furnishing of these spaces. For a fuller description of court life and domestic life we should refer to old Javanese literature. The scene we derive from these sources is one where people were seated – as some still are nowadays – on wooden floors or on mats made from various fibres like the 'Tikar' of pandanus leaves or 'lampit' of rattan (rotan) reeds. Only the King in his audience hall would be seated on a 'singgasana' or lion-throne, a raised platform on lion shaped legs, made of wood covered with ivory panels or with beaten precious metal.

The term used in old Javanese is of Sanskrit origin and so it seems the design is an Indian import.

Also missing from Odorico's account are the ubiquitous 'dulangs' made of wood or of bronze still seen in Sumatra, the Celebes, Java and Bali. These are plates on stands, sometimes with covers, used to present food, gifts and offerings in rituals, also believed to have been introduced from India.

Upholstered Biedermeyer-style settee in contemporary setting with carved backrest and apron. Front legs are gently splayed. Framed portrait by Miguel Covarrubias. Java, 19th century.

The Muslim kingdoms
(16th–19th century)

Islam came with Indian traders, first to northern Sumatra in the 13th century and later to Java in the 15th century. The architecture was basically the same as that of the Majapahit period, resembling the style still to be seen in the 'kraton' palace of Cirebon. Even the mosques were based on a traditional Javanese design, but with a new function. So was the furniture, though some new types were introduced such as the chair or 'kursi' and 'tahta' throne, both of which are Arabo-Persian words. A totally new piece of furniture found in mosques was the 'mimbar' or preacher's pulpit, which all over Indonesia is made of wood and finely carved with floral motifs and Arabic calligraphy, quoting verses from the Koran. Prayer carpets or mats were already used in mosques and homes and so were Koran book-stands (rekal).

The thrones of the Javanese sultanates of Surakarta and Yogyakarta, from the 17th till the 19th century, were transformed into backless stools made of wood covered with ivory, gold and silver leaf and set in the great audience hall or 'pendapa'. Rulers would sit erect on these stools for it was believed that a king should not lean on anything.

Most other people still sat on the floor on mats made of rattan reed or pandanus leaves. Some of these mats were lined with painted textiles or additionally woven with gold or silver thread to provide additional status.

The first piece of furniture used in ordinary homes at that time would have been a wooden chest in which people stored valuables such as heirlooms, wedding garments and, surprisingly, rice. These originally came from Syria or India, and were probably brought back from pilgrimages to Mecca.

The north coast of Java or 'Pasisir' was the first region to be exposed to the influences from China to its north, from India in the west and later from Europe.

The Arrival of the Europeans
(16th–19th century)

The Portuguese (16th century)

In 1511 the Portuguese from Goa on the western coast of India conquered Melaka (Malacca), an important Muslim Malay trade emporium in the straits which, in turn, afforded them access to the Indonesian archipelago with its famed Spice Islands, the Moluccas. A whole new phase of cultural exchanges commenced in Indonesia, especially on the island of Java.

The Portuguese brought many European innovations with them in dress and food and the technical terms from their language were adopted by almost all cultures in the archipelago, including Malay and Javanese.

Although one is unaware of any genuine Portuguese furniture found in Indonesia from this period, the Malay word 'meja', meaning table, was originally a Portuguese term. It seems that this was basically medieval in style with ornamentation of European origin carved by craftsmen in India. It was this basic design that was first adopted by the Dutch in India and then introduced to Indonesia. The term Indo-Portuguese was coined in England to describe that first style of 17th century furniture found in India, Sri Lanka and Indonesia.

While the Portuguese were busy extending their trade network from Goa in India and Malacca in the Malay peninsula, as far as Thailand, Vietnam and China and Japan in the north and the Moluccas in the eastern isles of Indonesia, the first Dutch ships appeared off the island of Java in 1595 and later took possession of all the island and its neighbouring archipelago.

The VOC – Dutch East India Company period (1602–1799)

Though the earliest Dutch merchants arrived in Bantam (West-Java) in 1595, the VOC, or Dutch East India Company, was founded only in 1602. It first occupied Amboyna in the Moluccas before founding in 1619 the city of Batavia on the ruins of Jacatra in west Java. Not until 1942 was Batavia renamed Jakarta as the capital of the Republic of Indonesia.

Right: Garden mirror framed by fretted appliqués woodwork, bordered with shelves displaying Shekwan ceramic ware.

Batavia became the first walled city of the archipelago and developed into an important trading centre in Asia, controlling all the VOC Factories and its network from Deshima in Japan through South-east Asia and India to the Persian Gulf and South Africa. On the island of Java, the VOC initially controlled the north coast, known as 'Pasisir', and through their involvement continued the development of a hybrid culture known as 'Pasisir' in every aspect of daily life and the arts and crafts on the basis of Javanese culture.

In the 18th century Batavia was widely renowned as the 'Queen of the East' and this can be seen in its architecture and certainly in its furniture, which has an original style based on European designs absorbing diverse elements from Chinese, Indian and Javanese cultures. The world expert on Dutch colonial furniture, J. Veenendaal, has suggested, quite rightly, calling this group of furniture Batavian (Veenendaal 2002) after the town which later became Jakarta.

The Batavian group of furniture of the 17th and 18th centuries comprises mainly chairs and armchairs, cabinets and chests, settees and daybeds, four-poster beds and tables. The wood used was chiefly teak, sometimes lacquered in black to suit Calvinistic taste but later also lacquered in red Chinese cinnabar and gilt, with gold leaf after the Chinese fashion. By the end of the 18th century this particular Batavian style influenced the creation of Javanese furniture known among the dealers as 'Kumpeni Jawa' or Javanese Compagnie.

The use of precious wood developed at the same time a style devoid of lacquer, to show off the original beauty of the grain in keeping with prevailing taste in Europe and China.

One has to imagine such furniture in the interiors of Batavian houses which were part European and part Chinese in construction, incorporating decorative elements from Java and India (Terwen-de Loos 1985).

The floors were covered with terracotta tiles made locally or with granite stone imported from Coromandel in India and from China, brought to Java as ballast on East-Indiamen. The use of teak wood for the upper floors imparted a warm feeling.

By the beginning of the 19th century, this whole new aesthetic in furniture would have been adopted first by the Javanese aristocracy on the Pasisir north coast of the island and later in the Mataram realm in the hinterland.

The beginning of the 19th century saw the continuation of furniture styles of the late 18th century. The production of items for the Javanese courts seems to have started in this period, comprising the so-called Kumpeni Jawa style inspired by late 18th century Batavian designs but with Javanese carving. This production continued until the mid-20th century.

The Javanese altar (petanen) found in traditional patrician houses or mansions is very often a four-poster or Chinese bed with canopy (krobongan) used in the past for rituals such as weddings and daily offerings which were not only common in the old court centres of Yogyakarta and Surakarta but also in all the regencies (kabupaten) of Java and Madura prior to the Second World War.

Palembang in south Sumatra was also the centre of an original style based on 18th century Batavian furniture but of smaller size, because it was proportioned for people accustomed to sitting on the floors of their vast houses on stilts. Requiring no chairs, their preference was for cabinets for wedding garments and chests of drawers lacquered with red cinnabar and enhanced with gold leaf using Chinese techniques.

The English East India Company period (1811–1815)

This was the period when English furniture in the Regency and Sheraton styles was first introduced to Java from India. The most ubiquitous piece of furniture of this type was the so called 'Raffles' chair, a classical armchair based on an Anglo-Indian Sheraton design developed in India and introduced to Java at the beginning of the 19th century. It became a very popular design and is produced and still known under that name today, all over Java.

Commenting on the 'Raffles' chair, the art historian Veenendal implies that the name of this particular armchair was not adopted from the name of Lieutenant-governor Stamford Raffles, who headed the British occupation of Java throughout the Napoleonic Wars in Europe, but rather is related to the word 'raffle' or lottery, which was in vogue during the 19th century in the main cities of Java (Veenendal 2001). He even suspects that the term was only coined in the early 20th century.

The Netherlands East-Indies period (1815–1942)

After the Napoleonic wars in Europe, the Netherlands became a kingdom and the Dutch regained their possessions in the archipelago, established as a genuine colony with the name Netherlands East-Indies.

The furniture designs developed during this period are mainly in the English Regency or Sheraton style, popularly known as the 'Raffles style'. They are mostly chairs, cupboards, cabinets and, above all, round tables of all sizes (0.50 metre up to 2.50 metres in diameter) with table tops made from a single piece of teak or Amboyna wood and sometimes Macassar ebony.

The most popular antique furniture in private collections in the major cities of Java, like Jakarta, Bogor, Semarang, Surabaya and Malang, comes from this period.

After the opening of the Suez Canal in 1869 more furniture was imported from Europe, which gave fresh inspiration for the cabinetmakers of Indonesia. This is how a type of Dutch Victorian style appeared in Indonesia.

The 19th century *Grand Salon* of Café Batavia, Jakarta, mirrors Indonesia's colonial past.

The imports included Carrara marble tops for tables of various sizes and for flooring and grand mirrors, with intricate frames made of gypsum. The bases of these tables were made locally, usually of teak.

The beginning of the 20th century (1900–1942)

At the end of the 19th century rattan wicker and bamboo furniture, imported initially from China and later made in Java, started a new vogue in light furniture which prevails today. This also coincided with the importation of Thonet furniture from Europe.

Because of their proximity to the large teak estates in Central Java, Semarang and Jepara became centres of carpentry, using precious woods specifically for the merchant classes of Pekalongan, Semarang and Surabaya.

The designs were possibly introduced from Dutch design magazines, for we start to find furniture in the Art Nouveau style but more often than not designs that remind us of the Wiener Werkstatte from Austria and the Darmstadt school from Germany (Schoppert 1997).

The Art Deco style, both in architecture and furniture design, became extremely popular on the island of Java, in cities as well as in the countryside. Bandung in west Java and Solo in central Java offer interesting adaptations of style (Tanjung 2001).

Even the rickshaws or 'becaks' of Tegal, Pekalongan, Semarang and Solo were incorporating Art Deco designs for their iron tubular frames.

Interestingly the rattan furniture style was influenced by modernist designs in the 30s (Terwen-de Loos 1985).

After the attack on Pearl Harbor at the end of 1941, the Japanese Imperial Army occupied Java for more than three years. Because of the war, there was little activity in the production of furniture in the archipelago. Curiously it is in the design of the 'Pasisir' north coast batik that Japanese elements of decoration can be found. This style goes under the Japanese name 'Djawa HooKooKai'.

The Indonesian Republican period
(1945 – present)

The Soekarno period (1945–1966)

The first president of the Republic of Indonesia, Soekarno, graduated as a civil engineer from the prestigious Polytechnic school in Bandung (now the Bandung Institute of Technology). One of his mentors was the Dutch architect, Wolf Schumacher, who taught him the rudiments of architectural design.

Because of his political activities, Soekarno has left behind very little in the way of architecture, other than a few buildings reputedly designed by him. He was also a talented watercolour painter, judging from paintings done during his banishment in Flores, which are today retained in private collections in Jakarta and in Solo.

In 1936–1942, while exiled in Bengkulu (Bencoolen) on the western coast of Sumatra, the young Soekarno was known to have apprenticed to a Chinese cabinetmaker as a furniture designer. Sadly no drawings or photographs showing the fruits of this collaboration exist.

When Soekarno and Hatta proclaimed independence for Indonesia in 1945, and after he had moved in 1949 to the former Palace of the Dutch Governor-Generals in Jakarta, Soekarno initiated the reconstruction of the interiors of all the presidential palaces.

He commissioned special furniture for the presidential palaces in Jakarta and Bogor in west Java, Yogyakarta in central Java and Tampak Siring in Bali, decorating these with paintings he had collected since before independence. The furniture produced was based on his designs in the late Art-Deco style, which remind us of the Parisian design of the 40s and 50s. This collection of furniture, paintings and decorative arts has been preserved by all subsequent Presidents to this day (Soekarnoputri 2004).

Soekarno was also committed to tourism and was directly involved in the designs and interiors of hotels he commissioned.

The opening in Jakarta of the Hotel Indonesia in 1962, for the Asian Games, was followed by the Ambarukma Palace Hotel in Yogyakarta and the Bali Beach Hotel in 1966, launching tourism development in Indonesia, especially in Bali and Jakarta. These inaugurated an International style for Indonesian furniture.

The Soeharto period (1966–1998)

Generally speaking Soeharto, the second President of the Indonesian Republic, was more concerned with the development of the country's economy. However, one of his priorities was to encourage foreign investment and continue developing tourism in Java and especially Bali.

With the Congress of the Pacific Area Travel Association, held in Jakarta in 1974, new hotels were inaugurated in Jakarta and Bali. These were instructed to incorporate as much as possible of the cultural elements from Indonesia's rich architectural and artistic heritage.

A new concept of hotel known now as the 'boutique hotel' started to evolve, initially on the island of Bali and then on Java. Pioneering this trend were the 'Tanjung Sari' hotel on Sanur beach and the 'Oberoi' on Kuta beach, both in Bali. In Java the 'Amanjiwo', close to Borobudur temple, deserves to be mentioned.

Interior designers drew their inspiration from the vast traditions of Indonesian furniture and decorative arts, which in turn saw a revival of the old cabinet making industries in Semarang, Jepara and Solo for wooden furniture and from Surabaya and Bandung for rattan and wicker furniture. The styles adopted were taken from Indonesian furniture designs incorporating the Javanese, Chinese and European styles from the 18th till the 20th century, and very rarely leaned towards the Indian traditions.

Right: Borobudur, the Buddhist monument in central Java, dates from the 8th century and is the largest stone structure in the world.

Conclusion

Too little is known about the many centres of furniture culture in outlying islands of the archipelago. More is known of Batavian furniture on the island of Java, thanks to the pioneering work of De Haan (De Haan 1922) and van de Wall (van de Wall 1939) whose interest in 17th and 18th century furniture found in the former Netherlands East-Indies stemmed from the tricentenary celebrations of the founding of the City of Batavia in 1919. Just prior to the Second World War a collection of this furniture was made by the Batavian Society for Art and Sciences. This collection was transferred first to the Old Batavia museum in 1939 and later, in 1974, incorporated into the Jakarta History museum housed in the restored 18th century Batavia City Hall in Jakarta Kota.

Last but not least, we owe much to the excellent research and publications of J. Veenendal (Veenendal 1985 and 2002).

Nothing similar has been done for Javanese and Madurese productions and even less for the very interesting Palembang furniture. The rustic Javanese furniture known by dealers as 'Primitif Jawa' furniture also deserves further study.

For some reason the Java Art Deco style has excited greater interest, although perhaps too artificial (Tanjung 2001), as has the so called 'Soekarno style' found in many established Jakartan houses and Presidential palaces (Soekarnoputri 2004).

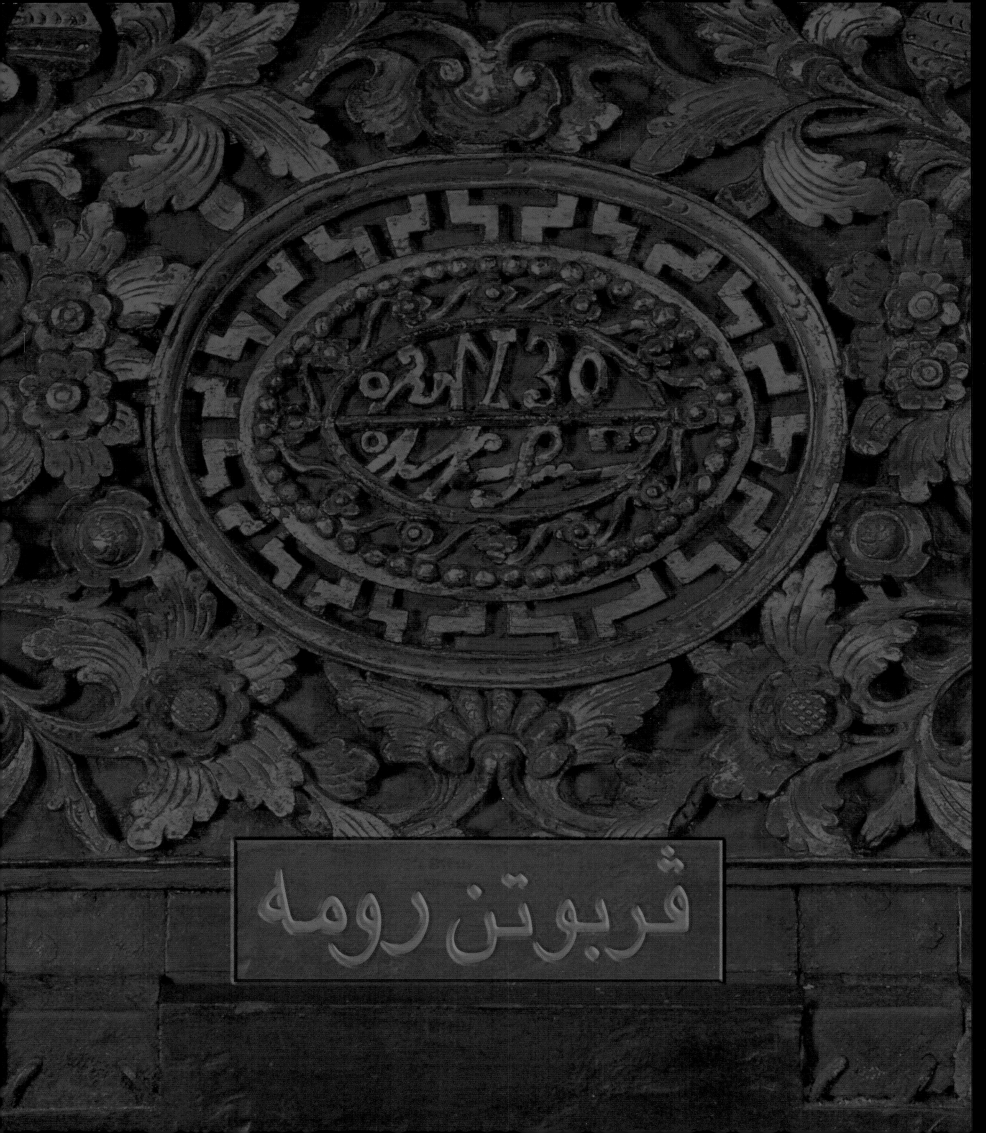

The interior of a contemporary Jakarta home displays as its centrepiece an 18th century *Lemari* (cupboard).

 Javanese dowry chest of teak wood. The interior of the carved lid bears the family crest.

 Lacquered dowry chest from Palembang, Sumatra. The interiors of the lid's three compartments are each stencilled with floral motifs. Trambesu wood. Early 19th century.

 Red and gold lacquered vanity mirror from Central Java. Floral details depict the sacred lotus – Buddhist symbol of purity and perfection.

 Dowry cabinet and chest of red lacquer with gilt carving from Palembang, Sumatra. Glass display panels indicate Dutch colonial influences.

 One of a pair of cupboards. Wedding armoires usually appear as pairs; with the taller male cupboard adorned with masculine symbols, such as weaponry, while the female cupboard is delicate, more finely carved and adorned with floral motifs. Glass panels indicate Dutch colonial influence.

 One of a pair of carved Palembang wedding cupboards with hand-painted gilded interiors. In this instance it is the female cupboard, adorned with lotus bulbs and floral motifs. Made of Tembesu wood – a south Sumatran hardwood.

 A large two-door, two-drawer *Lemari* (cupboard) from Central Java. The tiara is lacquered in red with highlights of gold leaf. An elegant X-stretcher connects the four-cabriole legs. Made of teak wood. 18th century.

Ornately carved wooden partition used as assembly room divider from the courthouse of the India Council of the Dutch East India Company. Teak wood. Batavia. 18th century.

A black with gold gilt bookcase of teak wood with four doors framing display vitrines. The pediment is adorned with figures representing *Truth* and *Justice*. The Batavia Council of Justice commissioned the armoire in 1748.

 Round table with single slat top made of ambon wood. Central column and base are of teak wood. Batavia. 19th century.

 Round table with single slat top of ambon wood. Central column and base are carved of teak wood. 19th century.

 Side table made of Indian Blackwood, with turned central column supported on tripod feet. Dutch colonial style. 17th century.

 Console with accentuated cabriole legs of green and gold finish made of teak wood. Central Java. 19th century.

 Circular table with ornately carved legs in red lacquer. The apron is decorated with the Garuda motif, sacred emblem of Indonesia. X-stretcher terminates in central finial that connects the four legs.

 Circular dining table with four cabriole supports and carved, central column attached to base. Teak wood. Dutch colonial style. 19th century.

Left: Red lacquered, two-door Javanese cabinet with ornately carved headboard of teak wood. The artist's easel displays a print of Borobudur, the 8th century Buddhist monument in Central Java.

Below: Red lacquered, two-door Javanese cabinet intended for storing *batik* or *ikat* textiles. Doors, frame and apron are embellished with floral motifs. Seated adjacent is a Balinese ceramic figure on side chest beneath a Balinese-style painting.

Left: Two-sectioned, black lacquered bureau from Palembang. Upper portion used to stow documents, while locks incorporated in the lower portion secure items of value. Pediment gable and lower apron are carved and lacquered in gold leaf.

Below: Dancing Balinese figures attend a red and gold lacquered *Lemari* (cupboard) with two doors and two drawers. The framed glass doors show the Dutch colonial influence. Gold leaf highlights the floral motif carved into the deep apron that seamlessly joins with cabriole legs.

SUMATRA

The great island of Sumatra is the third largest in Indonesia and the fifth largest in the world. Formed by a range of mountains which includes 15 active volcanoes, the island's principal exports are oil, natural gas and rubber. Sumatra stands at the crossroads of Asia, and was once covered in dense rainforest and inhabited by elephants, tigers, rhinos, gibbons, and orangutans.

Lacquered bureau with highly polished open plan writing surface. Rear section designed for the orderly filing of documents. H-stretcher connects with legs ending in ball and claw. Batavia. Late 18th century.

Two-drawer, Dutch colonial desk with writing surface and drawers edged in blackwood. Legs turned in twine motif connect with pronounced X-stretcher of same design. Made of makassar wood. Batavia. 18th century.

Two-drawer Dutch colonial writing table. Turned legs connect with pronounced X-stretcher. Made of ambon and ebony wood. Late 17th century.

 High-backed dining chair with prominent central back splat. Embellishments on backrest and apron are highlighted in gold leaf. Cabriole legs terminate in ball and claw. Seat is of woven cane. Batavia. 1750.

 Ornate lacquered armchair with seat of woven cane. Open work backrest is crested with peacock emblem. The four legs are steadied by a raised X-stretcher culminating in a central finial. Batavia. 18th century.

 Lacquered armchair made of teak wood. Backrest supports upholstered brocaded cushion. The seat is of woven cane. Commissioned by the Dutch East India Company. Batavia. Early 18th century.

 Corner chair. Frame and legs are of ambon wood, with panelled backrest and seat of ebony. Legs of twine motif connect with square stretcher. Batavia. 18th century.

 Conference chair with curved backrest and seat of woven cane. Teak wood. Batavia. 19th century.

 Chinese-style armchair with curved backrest and cane seat. Front leg, which terminates in ball and claw displays shell motif – insignia of royalty and is highlighted in gold leaf. 18th century.

 Chippendale style high-backed chair with central back splat support. Backrest and seat of cane matting. Batavia. 18th century.

JAVA

Indonesia's most populated island, Java, is situated between Sumatra and Bali. Its capital is Jakarta, also the capital of Indonesia. About half the province is under cultivation, the rest being densely forested. Major commercial crops include rubber, coffee, tea, sugar, quinine, tobacco, cacao, and timber. The population is predominantly Muslim, and includes people of Javanese, Sundanese and Madurese origin.

Settee of moulded wood of gold and lacquer polish with single matted cane seat. Front legs are splayed and upturned. Influenced by Biedermeyer or Empire style. Madura. East Java. 18th century.

Portuguese-style settee with intricately carved backrest pediment and apron. Seat is of cane matting. Two X-stretchers connect to, and steady, all six legs. Early 18th century.

Five-sectioned settee from the Governor-General of Batavia's palace. Seat is of double-sided woven cane in two partitions. Six front legs terminate in ball and claw and are connected by a central stretcher. Made of ambon wood. 18th century.

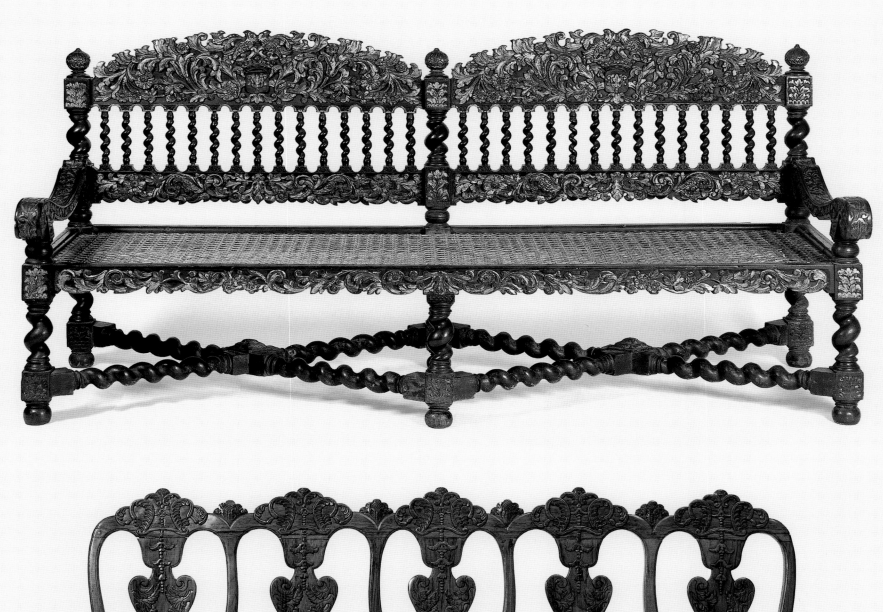

 Ecclesiastical chair, commonly found in monasteries and convents. Legs, front, side and back stretchers and backrest feature twine motif. Cane seat. Mullaca. 17th century.

 Blackwood armchair with crested pediment and ornately carved apron. Cane seat. Twine motif appears on legs, front, and side and back stretchers. Batavia. 18th century.

 Blackwood chair with carved backrest and cane seat. Legs and stretchers are decorated with twine motif. Batavia. Circa 1700.

Sidoarjo settee from East Java. Backrest pediment and front apron are elaborately carved. Ebony wood. Batavia. 18th century.

Blackwood settee with hard wooden seat. Crested pediment and front apron ornately carved and centred by lotus motif. X-stretcher connects all four legs. Java. 19th century.

Settee of teak wood with matted cane seat and carved, crested pediment and armrests. Stretchers with twine motif embrace all four legs. Java. 19th century.

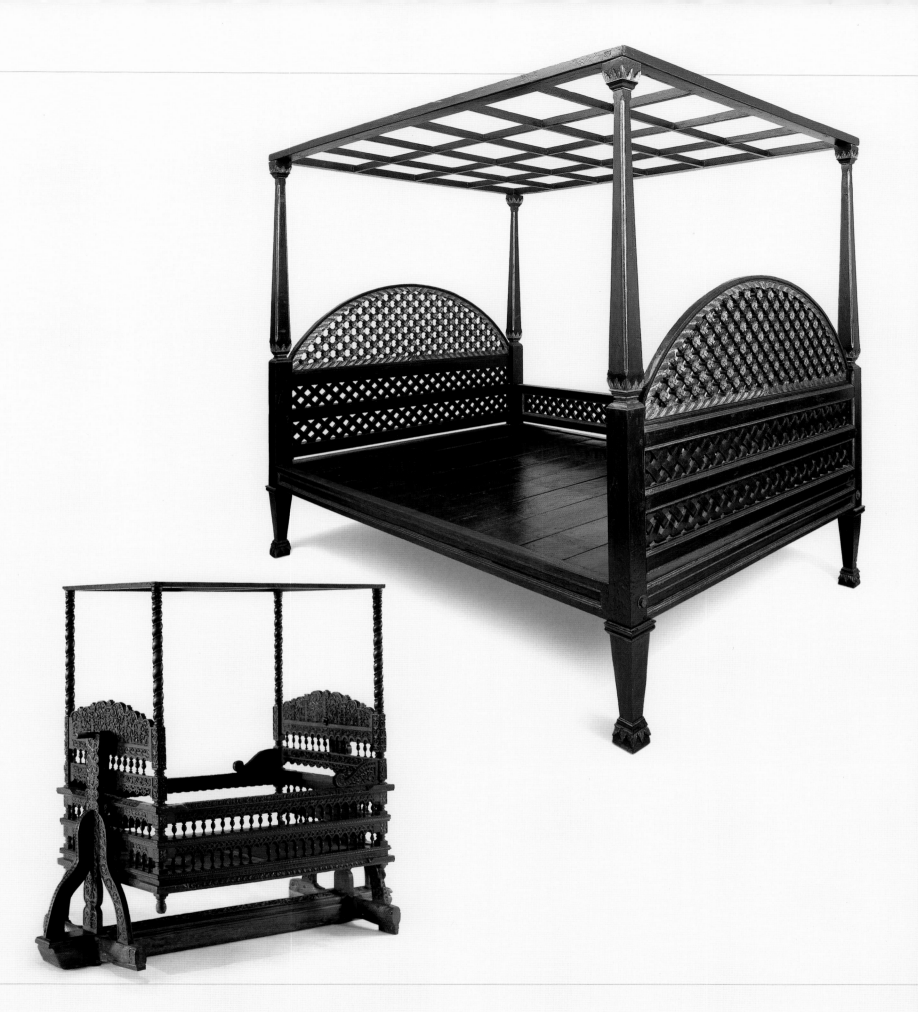

Left: Rural Chinese-style canopy bed fitted with mosquito netting. Bed, headboard and apron are embellished with floral motifs of green and gold lacquer. Java. 19th century.

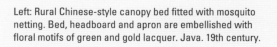
Four-poster bed of gilt and painted teak wood. Headboard and footrest are carved with identical gilt latticework. Madura. Early 19th century.

Four-poster rocking cradle with low-relief carving. Renaissance style. Teak wood. Batavia. Early 18th century.

Carved door panels from Pekalongan, Central Java. Decorated entrance to a Javanese home presents a formal welcome. The swastika and lotus emblems denote Buddhist and Hindu influences. Teak wood, with gilt and gold leaf highlights. 19th century.

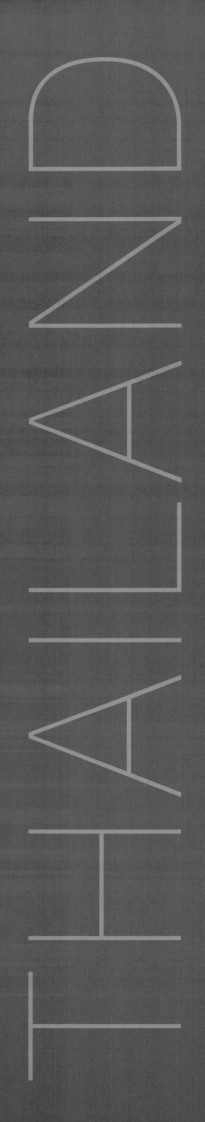

THAILAND

Squeezed like a shell in a nutcracker by neighbouring territories, with whom it successively waged war or forged alliances, Thailand has remained a unified kingdom since the mid-14th century. The only Southeast Asian country never taken over by a European power, it established a constitutional monarchy through bloodless revolution in 1932 and even managed to secure its neutrality, and preserve its Buddhist faith, when the rest of Southeast Asia was overrun by the Japanese in World War Two. Extending through 514,000 square kilometres of mountainous jungles and pagoda-strewn, temple-scattered rice fields, it maintains 4,863 kilometres of frontier with Burma, Cambodia, Laos and Malaysia.

Thai household chattels, including storage cabinets and platforms for sitting or sleeping, were traditionally constructed without legs.

On June 24, 1939 the Government of Siam, the only nation in Southeast Asia that had never been colonised by a foreign power, formally changed the country's name to Thailand, meaning "Free Land".

It was a name hard-earned, for Thailand had avoided annexation by *farangs* (foreigners) only through playing delicate games of astute diplomacy, pitting one rival European power against another and leaving their acquisitive, outstretched arms grasping at thin air.

As *LIFE* Magazine put it, in July 1939, "Only the canny rule of King Chulalongkorn in the late 19th century saved Siam from being swallowed by Britain and France, like the rest of Southeast Asia and the Malay peninsula".

But the game of evading colonial hegemony had commenced much earlier. It was King Nairi's resistance to Dutch aggression, in the 16th century, which laid the foundations for the Thais' prolonged but always victorious struggle to avoid European domination, and which allowed Thai civilisation to flourish unimpeded and largely unalloyed by the European influence that infiltrated other Asian cultures.

Inevitably, in a region of the world where such a patchwork of crowded territories shared common boundaries, coastlines, rivers, religions and migratory origins, there was an element of osmosis, of certain architectural styles and cultural values percolating through and infusing their neighbouring environments.

But in the main, despite occasional cross-border hostilities with Burma and Cambodia, Thailand remained surprisingly whole and sacrosanct, and no one deserves greater credit for that individuality than King Chulalongkorn.

Anna Leonowens, in her book *The English Governess at the Siamese Court* paints a striking portrait of his father, from whom Chulalongkorn inherited so much of his sagacity. She described King Mongkut as "a natural king among the dusky forms that surrounded him, the actual ruler of that semi-barbarous realm, and the prime contriver of its arbitrary policy.

Black, but comely, robust, and vigorous, neck short and thick, nose large and nostrils wide, eyes inquisitive and penetrating, his was the massive brain proper to an intellect deliberate and systematic".

"Well found in the best idioms of his native tongue, he expressed strong, discriminative thoughts in words at once accurate and abundant. His only vanity was his English, with which he so interlarded his native speech, as often to impart the effect of levity to ideas that, in themselves, were grave, judicious, and impressive".

Her description of King Mongkut set the tone for the much-loved Rogers and Hammerstein musical *The King and I*, which so aroused the indignation of Thai censors that they banned the film version from ever being shown in Thailand. They were principally offended by the portrayal of King Mongkut as "a youngish temperamental, despotic and irrational ruler, whom Anna Leonowens could easily influence".

"In real life", they averred, "King Mongkut was already approaching sixty at the time that Anna Leonowens arrived and was a truly respected and sensible monarch while Anna Leonowens was merely an English teacher to some of his children and female members of the court. The impact of Anna Leonowens during her five years service was so insignificant that her name was mentioned in King Mongkut's correspondence only once, when he described her as rather 'nosy'".

Other than the king himself, what seems to have made the greatest impression on the prim English governess was Thai architecture. She describes a building on an island near her allotted home as "perhaps the most unique and graceful object of architecture in Siam; shining like a jewel on the broad bosom of the river, a temple all of purest white, its lofty spire, fantastic and gilded, flashing back the glory of the sun, and duplicated in shifting, quivering shadows in the limpid waters below".

If architecture represented the apogee of Thai art, its furniture lay at the core, for both were unmistakably the products of the same aesthetic in regard to proportions, embellishments and finial ornamentation.

Previous page: The gracefully carved, gilt roof-ends of the Thai National Museum, Bangkok, built in 1874.
Opposite page: (Upper) Manicured lawns of the Maruekatayawan Palace, constructed by His Majesty King Vajiravudh, Rama VI in 1923. (Lower left) Classic architecture of the Lana-style Wat Phra That Bang Phuan in Chinag Mai, dating from 1498. (Lower right) The eaves of high-pitched roofs frequently took the form of protective nagas.

From Palace and Monastery to Private Home: A Short History of Thai Furniture

Pitya Bunnag

Before the mid 19th century furniture, with its English connotations, was unknown to the Thais. No word existed in the Thai vocabulary to convey the meaning of furniture, at least not before 1873. There is no such definition in the *Dictionary of the Siamese Language*, by D.B. Bradley (Bradley 1873), while in *The Comprehensive Anglo-Siamese Dictionary* by Samuel J. Smith, of 1901, furniture in English is translated into Thai as *khuang ruan* (household components).

Whatever basic apparatus was available to the Thais for home usage consisted of mats, boxes, drinking pots or elevated trays (*tok, toa*), but these were considered household utensils and not strictly furniture, for they had neither the function nor qualification of actual furniture. They were just mobile implements. The word *khuang ruan* (house components) remains in use as the modern Thai term for furniture. It originally implied the components of a house, such as pillars, posts, beams, or rafters, and since furniture is also a component of the house, it can in a broad sense be considered as *khuang ruan*.

King Rama V went to Europe in 1897, and again in 1907, and in his memoirs he described chairs, tables, curtains, including paintings and sculptures, as *khuang ruan*. At present it is the trend to borrow the English word furniture, without translation into Thai, to convey movable contents of any given room, such as chairs, tables, stools, cabinets etc.

There are two main reasons why Thais had limited home furniture in their culture, at least before approximately the mid 19th century. They considered furniture firstly as unsuitable and secondly as unnecessary. The point of unsuitability is accounted for by the fact that most houses were constructed of rattan and bamboo and could therefore not suitably sustain furniture. That it was also deemed unnecessary resulted from the very structure and arrangement of Thai houses, which in themselves provided and served as furniture.

Van Vliet, the acting Director of the Dutch East India Company (VOC), wrote in his *Description of the Kingdom of Siam 1638*:

"The houses of the mandarins and rich men are made of wood; the wide walls and front are provided with panels and the roofs are covered with red earthen tiles. . . . But the common and poor people live very poorly in reed and bamboo houses. The roofs are covered with cocos leaves or bad tiles, the floor of the houses is usually 4 to 6 feet above the ground, and the houses have no story or garret. Most times there is a front and a back door, but these are far from being good. Their sleeping rooms and resting places are bad, without any decoration and without curtains; the people sleep on stitched mattresses . . . ".

John Crawfurd, who visited Bangkok 187 years later, in 1835–36, wrote in his journal:

"The useful architecture of the Siamese is in a very humble state of advancement. The inhabitations of the lower orders consist always of simple and perishable materials, suitable enough, perhaps, to their climate, and certainly so to their poverty and incapacity of extending the sphere of their enjoyments. . . . the principal material employed in them being the bamboo, and the leaf of the Nipa palm (Nipa fruticans). I could not learn that solid materials, either of stone, or brick and mortar, were employed anywhere in the construction of the habitations of peasantry. The houses of the chiefs are most commonly of the same frail materials and in artificial structure as those of the peasantry, but we found a few at the capital constructed of brick and mortar, and roofed with tiles".

Visitors to the upper floor landing of the home of Jim Thompson, the legendary founder of the Thai Silk Company, are greeted by a two-door red lacquered cabinet and a glimpse of the dining room.

Bamboo and Nipa

The common, the poor or the lower orders mentioned above, made up the majority, at least 98% of the Thai population. But one must reflect that the caustic observations of both Van Vliet and John Crawfurd are based on western living standards. Nevertheless, because a house constructed of bamboo and of perishable materials clearly cannot hold much of a heavy load, too many personal effects, let alone furniture, would cause the entire flimsy structure to collapse. Moreover, the floors of primitive homes are made of split bamboo tied to bamboo joists; thus any article with protruding legs would simply penetrate the frail floor. This is the main reason why we find that most Thai household chattels, storage cabinets, sitting or sleeping platforms were constructed legless, as well as being light in weight and small in configuration.

The elevated trays (*tok, toa*), which form an integral part of Thai life and are a version of Thai table, are also made of bamboo, lacquered bamboo, wood or, if affordable, metal. They are light and have a circular base instead of pointed legs in order to distribute the weight evenly onto the floor, thus not causing any embarrassing mishaps. Boxes too are constructed legless, whereas mats are the essential equipment for reclining or sleeping on uneven and rudimentary floors, be they of affordable and desirable wooden floor boards or, as in most cases, of split bamboo.

As for royalty, the elite and the nobility, who made up barely 2% of the Thai population, they were no different when seen through the eyes of Western merchants, missionaries or diplomats. As van Vliet observed, "The noble, rich, and poor alike do not need more furniture than is necessary for sleeping, cooking and eating".

Nicolas Gervaise, a French missionary to Ayutthaya in 1683 wrote in his *Histoire Naturelle et Politique du Royaume de Siam*:

"In general, we have no house in our country that equals theirs in simplicity of their furnishings. Even in the rooms of their most magnificent palaces there are no tables, chairs, or wall-hangings, but only a few Chinese or Japanese cabinets, some badly arranged pieces of porcelain, a few Persian carpets to cover the floor, and some silk cushions, which are placed in the corner of the room with some mats made of rushes or rice-straw. These mats, which they spread out when they wish to sleep, serve as beds, and they cover themselves with a pagne. . . . They never use sheets and the cleanest and best house people have only a light cotton mattress on a little rush bed with muslin net over it".

The French diplomat Simon de La Loubère put it succinctly when he concluded that the Siamese were "rich in a general poverty" in their dress, housing, and diet.

It would seem therefore that furniture is not a necessity among the Thais in their daily life, since it is the custom of the Thais to sit on the floor. Moreover Thai houses are divided into strata, befitting the status of each social level.

Furniture as Status Symbol

Furniture, besides having the basic physical function of serving the bodily posture and providing comfort and convenience, also has a secondary, equally important function. Furniture serves as a status symbol, to indicate the owner's superiority in society. However, this secondary function of supremacy seems to have rubbed against the grain of the original law of the land.

The Thai Palatine Law or *kot monthienban* forbade, on pain of death and confiscation of property, any private association between the *khunnang* (officials, nobles) bearing *sakdina* rank of between 1,600 and 10,000, as designated by the King. This law presumably was enforced during the reign of King Prasathong in the 17th century. With his first hand information, van Vliet recorded:

"His Majesty (King Prasathong) has issued strict orders that all the powerful Mandarins (except when indisposed) appear at the Court each day. In addition, he has prohibited the Mandarins from visiting each other in their houses, and he has stipulated that they consult each other only in public places when everyone can hear what they have to say".

The master bedroom of the Jim Thompson House.
The traditional Thai reclining platform has been converted
into a western-style bed. The wall hangings depict Vessantara
Jataka tales. The stone figure is of the Goddess Una.

Therefore, to be on the safe side and to avoid any slight, it became the custom and practice for officers of nobility to avoid visiting each other's homes. Thus to exhibit or flaunt one's treasure and wealth, by using furniture as a medium, seemed to defeat the whole purpose of acquiring status symbols, because no one of any social standing would ever officially have the opportunity to appreciate or to admire their neighbour's acquired furniture, which would be seen only by their own families, visiting relatives perhaps and servants or slaves.

It would therefore have been quite unwise to flaunt any form of wealth, especially to the tyrannical and avaricious government, for one's days would surely be numbered if seen to be boasting. Because of this insecure social situation, filled with suspicion, fear and anxiety, furniture however magnificent had insignificant value for the Thais during the Ayutthaya Period, which spanned early Thai history's greatest era of international trade from 1350–1767.

The Richest Emporium

Ayutthaya's role as a port made it one of Southeast Asia's richest emporia. The port of Ayutthaya was an entrepôt, an international market place where goods from the Far East could be bought or bartered in exchange for merchandise from the Malay/Indonesian Archipelago, India, or Persia, not to mention local wares or produce from Ayutthaya's vast hinterland, let alone any other kind of material possessions.

The Thais, be they rich or poor, hardly considered furniture an asset, unlike gold, silver, ornaments and especially textiles, which could be stowed, packed away or buried for the rainy day, as stability one day became uncertainty the next. The only safe means during the Ayutthaya Period, to flaunt one's wealth lay with those granted privileged rights by the Crown. Eventually this attitude of assimilation became the benchmark for Thai culture during the Ayutthaya period, when one was at an early age made aware of one's station in life and taught not to place oneself above the station of others, especially not those of superior rank.

The highest and most honourable recognition the *khunnang* derived from the king would be their titles, honorific names and the right to wear uniforms befitting their status. They received no fixed income or remuneration. The most powerful *khunnang* were rewarded with manpower rather than cash or material assets. To secure the throne, the 17th century kings of Ayutthaya attempted to increase their own revenue, and at the same time prevent families of nobility from becoming too powerful. The *Khunnang's* wealth inevitably consisted in part of what they could extract from their posts of influence by way of 'gifts'. With their titles they also received marks of honour and distinction in the material form of elaborately decorated or embossed betel boxes and a fixed number of retainers.

The Trappings of Rank

The rank that all mandarins held in the kingdom was evident whenever they appeared in public, not only from the form of their *boussettes* (betel set) or the design and material of the circlets that crowned their caps . . . but also the fixed number of retainers permitted. The *boussette* of the highest rank, *ocya* was much more finely wrought than those of the rest, and the golden circlets they wore like crowns around their pointed caps were spangled with floral designs and rosettes.

The second rank of nobility was that of the *ocpras*. Their *boussettes* were of gold, but less finely adorned than those of the *ocya*, and the gold circlets round their caps were decorated with leaf-work only. The third rank of nobility was the *oclouangs*. Their *boussettes* were of silver, though decorated with festoons and boughs, and the circlets round their caps were a mere two inches wide, with much less handiwork than those of the *ocpras*. The *okcounes* and *okmunes* comprised the fourth and fifth classes of nobility. Their *boussettes* and circlets round their caps were simply of plain gold or silver.

The nobles and mandarins, and also their wives, were accompanied by 10 to 40 slaves, male and female (the number determined in accordance with their status); the elite and wealthy would promenade with ample servants, while the common men and women were accompanied by one to three servants at most.

Furniture as a means of comfort, or status as in the western sense, did not play a role in Thai culture. Thus there was no Thai cabinet, no Thai chair nor Thai table, no Thai bed, Thai screen, not even a Thai carpet. If need be, in more contemporary times the Thai might resort to western imported furniture for substitution. As Choisy, an envoy of King Louise XIV of France to the court of King Narai of Ayutthaya wrote in his memoir in October 1685:

"And at midday I reached the first of the seven houses built for the Ambassador. Everywhere there are Chinese beds, Persian carpets, Japanese screens". Gervaise, a contemporary French missionary confirmed: ". . . but only a few Chinese or Japanese cabinets, some badly arranged pieces of porcelain, a few Persian carpets to cover the floor".

The alternative to accumulating assets during their lives was earning merit, in hopes that what they deposited in this life would eventually be rewarded in the next life, including interest and dividend. In Buddhist teaching, the law of karma teaches that responsibility for unskilful actions is borne by the person who commits them. Most would like to be reborn in the time of Maitreya, the future Buddha, somewhat equivalent to the land of Arcadia.

For this spiritual reason, most so-called Thai furniture of quality, such as scripture cabinets, monk preaching platforms, low tables and lacquered screens etc., are to be found in monasteries. Though they may cosmetically be Thai in appearance, as witnessed by lacquer finish, gold leaf adornment and traditional Thai patterns, motifs or painted scenes from the classics, their construction and design are undoubtedly Chinese in origin, as the finest carpenters were immigrant Chinese cabinetmakers.

There is one item of Thai furniture that needs special mention. It is a low table, or rather stool, a bed with inward-curved cabriole legs ending in lion claws. These recliners or beds are not common to the average Thai home but reserved for the nobility and bearers of the high rank of *sakdina*. Presumably this practice came into use in the Bangkok Period, because evidence of them is not yet apparent in the Ayutthaya Period.

The Bangkok Period

The Bangkok Period (1767–1932) originated after the Thais recovered from their defeat by the Burmese at Ayutthaya, under the brilliant military leader Taksin (1767–1821), who had slipped away from besieged Ayutthaya and, starting with a handful of followers which quickly grew into an army, organised a resistance to the Burmese invaders, driving them out of the land after a long and arduous war. Assuming the royal title, he abandoned the ruined state of Ayutthaya and founded a new capital further south in the delta at Thon Buri, a fortress town across the river from modern Bangkok. By 1776 Taksin had reunited the Thai kingdom.

The size, height and types of ornamentation of these recliners and beds during the Bangkok period would depend on the status of the users. Those with lion claws or five-clawed dragon feet would be restricted to members of the royal family. However early they are documented in Thai usage, there is still nothing ethnically Thai about them, as they remain typically Chinese in design, joinery and production.

By the early Bangkok Period, the situation of the ruling elite changed somewhat. From the reign of King Rama II (1809–24) onwards, the administration fell into the hands of the nobility, most related to each other by marriage, who were therefore powerful enough to elect their own kings.

The turning point of Thai home furniture begins approximately at this time, the mid 19th century, with the reign of King Rama IV (1851–68) better known as King Mongkut, who at the age of 20 had been ordained as a Buddhist monk. Before ascending the throne he spent 27 years in the monkhood. This gave him the opportunity to tour the country, discovering the people's needs and learning much from foreigners who had begun to reside in Siam.

In particular Mongkut learned English from missionaries, which he later used to his advantage to correspond personally with Queen Victoria and President Lincoln. His reign coincided with western imperialist global colonisation, under the pretext of civilising backward nations – though as the Thais saw it, the real motive was something quite different. Realising the grave situation this posed for his country, Mongkut wrote to Phraya Suriwongse Vayavadhana, the then Siamese ambassador in Paris:

"Supposing we were to discover a gold mine in our country … enough to pay for the cost of a hundred warships; even with this we would still be unable to fight against them (the Europeans), because we would have to buy those very same warships and all the armaments from their countries. They can always stop the sale of them whenever they feel that we are arming ourselves beyond our station. The only weapons that will be of real use to us in the future will be our mouths and our hearts, constituted so as to be full of sense and wisdom for the better protection of ourselves". In order to avoid the calamity of conquest by the western colonial powers, it was necessary for the Thais to adjust and to reform themselves in accordance to the western standards of civilisation.

Avoiding the Threat of Colonisation

Because of these western undercurrents threatening his nation, the King made many changes to the archaic customs of the country. One of the first royal proclamations concerned the nobility, who had hitherto presented themselves naked to the waist in His audience. Henceforth, the King decreed, they must appear fully clothed. This act is contrary to Thai custom, as subordinates when in the presence of their seniors or masters, should not have the upper part of the body concealed by clothing. This probably derived from reasons of security, as weapons could be hidden under the garments. But as this archaic Thai practice was no longer in accordance with King Mongkut's views of western standards of civilised nations, it had to be changed by an act of law.

For the good of the nation, King Mongkut dressed himself in western uniform, wearing western regalia, seated on a western chair to be officially photographed. As the photograph was the most advanced medium of the day, he distributed his image freely among kings, queens, and emperors of Europe in order that they should view him as the king of civilised Siam. Sir Robert Hermann Schomburgk, the first British Consul directly appointed by London, arrived in Siam in 1857 and recorded that King Mongkut summoned his two brothers who, like the rest of the entourage, approached the King in a crawling posture. "The King motioned them however to rise up and be seated in his presence on chairs".

It is said that King Mongkut even compiled the much disputed and controversial stone inscription No. 1, known as the *Ramkhamhang* Inscription, in order that the world might comprehend – in Mongkut's own words – "The long and uninterrupted history of Siam".

Among the royal gifts that King Mongkut sent to Emperor Napoleon III was a set of knives, forks and spoons made of gold inlaid with diamonds and rubies. It was his subtle way of insinuating that the manner of dining of the Siamese was not inferior to the French, though he himself still dined, as did his subjects, with his fingers, befitting the Siamese manner.

The decrees implemented by King Mongkut are but skimmed milk masquerading as cream, all for the survival of the nation of Siam. And survive it did, as witnessed by Lord Clarendon's letter dated February 1858 to King Mongkut.

"I doubt not, assure Your Majesty of the sincere desire which is felt by the Queen and Her government for the independence and welfare of Your Kingdom, and for the perpetuation of friendly connection between Siam and the British Empire".

Emulating the Farangs

During King Mongkut's reign, trade and commerce increased quite considerably. Those who enjoyed the direct benefits were the crown and a handful of nobles. Unlike the Ayutthaya Period, they were now able to ostentatiously flaunt their wealth to their heart's content, safe from obstruction or persecution. Exotic goods were ordered from catalogues by shipment from Europe. They comprised mostly scientific or household instruments, such as barometers, thermometers, clocks of countless design, pocket watches, paraffin lamps, candlesticks, pistols, water filter pots, etc.

At this time, the array of European furniture was not yet readily acceptable to the Thai upper class. But there was a type of cabinet that reflected the general taste of Thai upper class society. That is the type of cabinet now modified with glass front panels. Actually, this form of cabinet is but an adaptation of the monastic scripture cabinet, originally derived from the classic Chinese book cabinet. Though Chinese in character and construction, it can somehow be seen as Siamese, for there is no such prototype in China. The purpose of having the transparent front doors was primarily to flaunt the owner's objects of value, since he was now no longer under threat to his life. And later the cabinet's evolution went a step further. Not only did the cupboard have front doors that were transparent, but the sides too were installed with glass panels.

The great impact of western architecture and furniture in Siam, as it was still known then, would come during the reign of King Mongkut's son, King Rama V (1868–1910), known as King Chulalongkorn. The education of his early days was entrusted to an American woman, Anna Leonowens, and later Captain John Bush. He enjoyed a long reign that allowed him to fulfil his father's plans and bring Siam to the point of modernity. He travelled to Singapore, Java, India and twice to Western Europe, intensifying his desire to continue the Westernisation of his kingdom.

Chulalongkorn made every effort to turn Bangkok into a western looking colonised city without necessarily becoming a western colony. He fully realised that "it is very hard to find no worse an enemy than the farangs (whites)", so he better play the game according to the rules. Neoclassic, Gothic Revival and Mansart styles of architecture were the themes of the day. European architects were commissioned to design palaces, mansions, monastic and public buildings, banks and bridges. Countless fittings and components ranging from doorknobs, window frames and hinges, flooring, railings, ornate lighting, slate tiles, marble toiletry etc. were all installed according to western architectural specifications, and had to be imported from Europe, for they were unknown in Siam.

Carl Bock, who visited Bangkok in 1881, wrote in his book *Temples and Elephants*, "The style (of the Chakr Kri Maha Prasat Palace) is a mixture of different schools of European architecture, the picturesque and characteristic Siamese roof, however being retained. The internal fittings of this palace are on a most elaborate scale, the most costly furniture having been imported from London at an expense of no less than £80,000. One of the features of the palace is a large and well-stocked library, in which the king takes great interest – all the leading European and American periodicals and newspapers being regularly taken in".

Fournereau noted that the gigantic cut glass chandelier hanging in the audience hall of the Chakr Kri Palace was from the Baccarat section of the 1878 World Exposition.

Detail of a dragon motif on the apron of a Thai reclining platform.

"No Such Thing as Siamese Chairs"

Émile Jottrand wrote in his diary in 1901 that "We noticed in the three pavilions a large number of Thonet chairs, this infallible indication of approaching civilisation, as there was no such thing as Siamese chairs".

Sitting on chairs was still a novelty to the Siamese, and a practice largely confined to royalty of prominence and powerful nobles on official occasions. Ordinary officers still sat on the floor. As for women, irrespective of their importance, they had no right to sit on any form of chair except when being photographed. The rest of the inhabitants still live in bamboo houses with thatched roofs and few pieces of household utensils essential for their living, as they have since the time of their forefathers.

Since 1857 there had been a tendency for the Thai elite to send their sons for education in England. In 1867, when Chao Phraya Suriwongse Waiyawat (Won Bunnag) went on an embassy to France, he left his son, Nai Toh (later Chao Phraya Suriwongse Watanasakdi) in England for education. By 1926, there were no less than 2,000 Thai students studying in England, whose number had recently included the crown prince Vajiravudh.

When Vajiravudh became king in 1910, he continued to lead the life and customs of an English gentleman he had absorbed during his time at school. Without fail, every night at eight he would dine by candlelight in his Bangkok residence, dressed appropriately in dinner jacket and tie. Contrary to his orchestrated and conflicting modes of extravagant living, he remained conscious of his western infused habits, for he wrote:

"Those Asians who adopt the custom and manners of *farangs* (whites), are like slaves trying to imitate their masters. . . . There are those who fashion themselves in the *farangs'* outfits, however badly tailored, hoping to impress and gain the respect of their *farang* comrades. But is that respectability sincere? Surely not, for it only creates the feeling of sympathy similar to what one feels toward a puppy that has been taught to sit upright on its hind legs. Whatever the puppy may think, it cannot replace a child. The reason we feel sympathetic toward the puppy is because it tries to imitate the human action. The most we could do is to pat its head and call it a clever dog".

There was an amazing transformation of life in only four decades after the reign of King Rama VI, when most Thais were still living in indigenous houses, to the mid-20th century when they preferred to live in furnished Western style houses and clothed in the Western manner. A remarkable role reversal has taken place. Today resident foreigners are more likely to be the ones living in fashionable vintage-style Thai houses, surrounded by ostensibly Thai furniture that subjects their creaking teak floorboards to undue stress, while the urban Thais themselves, having largely turned their backs on all that, inhabit brick, mortar and concrete homes, or high-rise apartments, in simulated western environments, high above their erstwhile canals and conspicuous traffic jams.

เครื่องเรือน

SUKHOTHAI

Thai governors who rebelled against the Khmers founded Sukhothai, the first Thai kingdom in 1238. Liberated from external aggression the province quickly expanded its cultural influence as the prowess of Thai artisans, sculptors, stonemasons and potters resulted in extensive trade with Cambodia and India. The boundaries of Sukhothai then stretched from Lampang to Vientiane in present day Laos, and south to the Malay Peninsula.

 Two-door carved lacquer and gilt scripture cabinet of Chinese style and construction. Panels depict door guardians standing on *Kilan,* a mystic animal. Donated by Wat Chandaran – Dhonburi 1918.

 Rare example of faux façade gold and black lacquer, *Lai Rod Nam* Buddhist scripture cabinet with protruding red pedestal resting on a low table with turned legs. The actual doors to the cabinet are on the obverse side. From Lampung. 19th century.

CHIANG MAI

The origins of Lanna lie on the Mekong River, where King Mengrai ascended the throne in 1259. Mengrai extended the realm from Laos to Lamphum, and founded the new capital of Chiang Mai. The Lanna Period flourished for over 200 years and its arts and literature rose to their peak in the 15th century. Ultimately its enviable economy was weakened as a result of protracted wars protecting itself against the successors of the Sukhothai.

Left: Finely carved two-door cabinet, gilded on three façades with apron terminating in cabriole legs. Intended for Dharma (principal of the cosmos) documents. Donated by Wat Ban Kling. Ayutthaya Period. 17th–18th century.

Tapered, two-door scripture cabinet carved with scenes from Vessantara Jataka tales. Gold leaf. Teak wood. Rottana Ko Sin Period.

Tapered, two-door, two-drawer black and gold lacquered scripture cabinet with carved openwork apron. Teak wood. Bangkok Period. Mid 19th century.

BANGKOK

Bangkok began as a small port community, called Bang Makok, 'place of olive plums', serving Ayutthaya, the capital of the nation, then known as Siam, until it fell to its northern invaders in 1767. A new capital was established at Thonburi on the western shore of the Chao Phraya River. Present day Bangkok comprises an old district of Thonburi which has long served as the gateway to Thailand, because of its advantageous location on a river flowing into the Gulf of Thailand.

Left: Scripture cabinet of gold and black *Lai Rod Nam* lacquer portrays scenes of the God Indra descending from heaven in his *Rata* – chariot on wheels – drawn by Erawan, the three-headed elephant, which treads majestically along corridors of attendants who pave its way with petals and prayers.

Tapered two-door, two-drawer gold leaf cabinet for the safekeeping of Buddhist manuscripts. Scenes depicted from the Mahajati Jataka, showing the Bodhisatta reborn as Vessantara to practice *parami*, the culture of giving alms. Ayutthaya Period. 18th century. Teak wood.

Tapered Tripitaka scripture cabinet with *Lai Rod Nam* black and gold lacquer. Doors depict scenes from Temiya Jataka, one of the previous lives of the Lord Buddha. Here Temiya tests his strength after a lifetime of deception as a cripple. He raises a chariot and hurls it over his head. Early Bangkok Period, 1820s.

 Left: A red and gilt two-door, two-drawer display cabinet with glass panels of Chinese design and construction. The apron terminating in ball and claw is finely carved and is highlighted in gold leaf. Bangkok Period. Mid 19th century.

 Tall glass vitrine altar cabinet displays images of the Lord Buddha. Elaborately decorated with mirrors and mother-of-pearl inlay. Ratannakosin Period.

 Scripture chest converted into display cabinet of glass panels. Finely executed figures are painted on the cabinet's sides and doorframes. Bangkok Period. Mid 19th century.

A modernised vitrine display cabinet with pronounced cabriole legs of *Lai Rod Nam* black and gold lacquer. This durable form of lacquer ware has evolved from the end of the Ayutthaya Period and is still employed on contemporary furniture today.

Left: Two-door, glass panelled, three-drawer display cabinet with elaborately carved diadem characteristic of Thai and Chinese cabinets of the late 19th – early 20th century. The cabinet stands on a lower table with carved apron ending with claw and ball feet. King Rama V Period.

Red gilt display cabinet with varied and stepped shelves behind westernised glass door panels. Elaborately carved tiara has Malay/Chinese influences. King Rama V Period.

Right: The splendid and spacious living room of the Jim Thompson House, with a reclining platform of carved
teak wood and an altar with an image of the Lord Buddha commanding centre stage. Scripture cabinets
stand sentry against polished teak walls. Close-up of platform (above) shows detail of a superbly carved leg,
terminating in claw foot and ball.

A rare and unique Thai reclining platform with gold gilt carved apron. The vertical line of joinery and florid decoration on the apron is distinctive of the Neo Classic European trend. King Rama V Period. Mid 19th century.

Right: Detail of a Thai authentic reclining platform. The leg ends in a dragon's five-clawed foot and ball — sign of royal patronage, as does the dragon motif on the apron. Joinery line at 45° signifies strong Chinese carpentry influence. Teak wood. Late 18th century.

Thailand has developed sophisticated equipment for riding elephants, hardly surprising in a country that has domesticated these animals for centuries and has made the elephant its national emblem. Today, elephant chairs, known as *howda*, are commonly converted into exotic home accessories.

Ceremonial *howda* of teak supports with seat of split rattan and frail railing interspersed with ivory.

The basic *howda* is a wide bench-like seat with raised sides and back, built over a yoke that is splayed to fit onto the elephant's back.

A canopied *howda* intended for royalty or the nobility on hunting expeditions. The chair itself is gilt-etched. The canopy is of bamboo supports with rattan shading and is lacquered in gold and red. King Rama V Period. Mid 19th century.

  Elaborately carved *Kan Chong* vanity case with adjustable mirror topped with carved diadem. The *Naga* head motifs symbolise water, which represents fluidity and abundance. Bangkok Period. Mid 19th century.

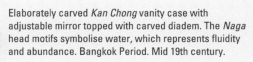 Vanity table with reclining, adjustable mirror, crested with carved tiara and decorated in gold leaf with *Naga* head motifs. Bangkok Period. Mid 19th century.

 Royal vetement (clothing) chest of *Lai Rod Nam* black and gold lacquer, a durable form of lacquer developed in the early Ayutthaya Period (1350–1766). The interior of the chest is lacquered in deep red contrasting tones.

A ceiling screen in the North Thailand – Burmese style. The screen depicts costumed mythical dancing figures, miming the ancient classics, performed for the royal court. Mandalay Period. Late 19th century.

Khmer Singha (lions) of granite stand guard on either side of carved door panels that once opened gracefully onto the inner courtyard of a Thai palace. Guardians of stone are commonly found at the entrances of temples, palaces and buildings of note throughout the cultures of Indo-China.

CHINA

Only slightly smaller than the United States of America, China encompasses 9,596,960 square kilometres and houses so many people – 1,306,313,812 by mid-2005 – that it accounts for one fifth of the world's population.

For centuries it remained in self-imposed isolation, the 'Great Within', outpacing the rest of the world in arts and sciences, but by the 19th and early 20th centuries the country was beset by civil unrest, major famines, military defeats, and foreign occupation. Today it is rising phoenix-like from the ashes of its recent history to regain its place as a paramount power.

Among the first of the world's great civilisations, China's embraced a social spectrum ranging from ultra extravagance to extreme poverty. It was so large and self-sustaining that it developed, very early in its history, an acute conviction of its own sufficiency and superiority, to the point where its imperial palace became known as "The Great Within".

China invented paper, gunpowder, matches, the compass, a seismograph to measure earthquakes, the umbrella, the wheelbarrow and much more. Early Chinese peoples conceived complex philosophies, created exquisite works of art and spawned great legends.

The Lungshan people of the Xia Dynasty, from 2100 to 1800 BC, were accomplished engineers, skilled in the fabrication of silk, working clay on the potter's wheel and constructing dwellings of baked brick. Their agriculture benefitted from their mastery of irrigation and flood control.

The resplendence of Chinese furniture lies in the marriage of design, elegance and simplicity with detail.

The Shang people who followed, spanning the years 1700 to 1027 BC, possessed bronze weapons and invented writing, the earliest examples of which were found on oracle bones used for divination. The Zhou, who supplanted them, introduced the concept of the Mandate of Heaven, under which only the strongest was worthy of the responsibility to govern.

The competition to assume that mandate led to the period known as the Warring States, a time of great philosophers and cultural flowering that produced Confucianism, Taoism, and Legalism. Of these, Legalism provided the foundation for the Qin, whose dynasty was next in succession, covering the relatively short time span from 221 to 207 BC.

The Qin ruler Shi Huangdi laid claim to being China's first true emperor, and standardised its language and writing, together with its currency and the measurement of axle length, to ensure that ruts made by cartwheels dictated roads of uniform width. He built the Great Wall to protect against invasions from the north and laid highways and irrigation canals throughout the country. He also ensured that when he died a terra cotta army of six thousand pottery soldiers was buried with him.

Despite all his accomplishments, Shi Huangdi was not popular. His public works and taxes imposed too great a burden on the people, while the nobility disliked him because he deprived them of their power and banned all books advocating forms of government other than his. The writings of the great philosophers of the Warring States were burned and more than four hundred opponents were executed.

When the brief-lived Qin Dynasty came to an abrupt end with Shi Huangdi's death, the Han Dynasty heralded a revival of Confucian ideals as the basis for more humane policies, a liberal approach to education and the establishment of the Silk Road as an open door to trade expansion.

In the subsequent turbulent age of the Three Kingdoms, China once again disintegrated into competing states, each of whose rulers remained determined to vanquish his rivals. From this troubled era emerged Ssu-ma Yen, who in 265 AD founded the Chin Dynasty, which was to prove the last of the early dynastic age.

The greater accomplishments of China's classical imperial dynasties were yet to follow, but already its furniture had made sufficient advances to lay the groundwork for one of the country's supreme art forms.

From engravings on stone and stamped brick, we learn that the custom of kneeling, or sitting cross-legged upon woven mats, has yielded accessories in the form of low tables, screens, and armrests. Examples of excavated lacquer furniture, dating from around 500 BC, demonstrate an aesthetic of minimalism and simplicity.

Here began the blending of artistic form with practical functionality – the common thread running throughout the long history of Chinese furniture.

Enduring Classicism of Chinese Furniture

Willy Wo-lap Lam

The well-known French critic, Odilon Roche, once wrote of furniture from the Middle Kingdom as a celebration of "simplicity, nobility and grandeur". For the Chinese historian Wang Shixiang, these eminently usable *objets d'art* were paragons of "purity, dignity and gravitas". The finely crafted chairs, coffers and cupboards have a Confucianist air of propriety about them. The pulse slows when one is seated on a Ming dynasty horseshoe back chair.

Classic Chinese furniture is today enjoying a strong revival of interest, both in Asia and the West. Though remaining eminently functional, chairs, coffers and cupboards are essentially works of art; a testament both to the natural beauty of wood grain and the understated elegance that can be achieved through contours and ornamentation.

What a triumph for the modern notion of economy of style and function! The most elegant of chairs are unupholstered. Their form tends to encourage the adaption of an upright posture. And indeed, what better manner could there be to slip into the Taoist way of simple commerce with nature as the seasons scroll past? And perhaps, reclining in a canopied bed with lattice work and flowing silk, one may begin to daydream like the Chinese philosopher Zhuang Zi, of man metamorphosing into a butterfly.

While the quasi-art objects are a testimony to eclecticism, the best works are harmonious marriages of the *yin* – the natural beauty of the wood grain – and the *yang*, the design and ornamentation. The vast range of classic Chinese furniture remains overwhelming. Collectors' items range from brushpots, cosmetic boxes and side tables to gilded wardrobes, lacquered cabinets and imperial thrones.

Consider for example a screen room divider that consists of panels, each of which bears different inlaid carvings. In the way of *trompe l'oeil*, it's a virtual landscape within the living room, or the detailed apothecary's cabinets (page 134 and page 135) which boast many small drawers each engraved with descriptive characters for the herbal remedies they contain.

The resplendence of Chinese furniture lies in the marriage of design, elegance and simplicity with detail. How does one ensure that the wood-grain pattern of the door panels of a cupboard or wardrobe perfectly matches that of its neighbours? One can lose oneself admiring the carvings alone, which come in free style, relief or openwork. Apart from floral and mythical creatures such as dragons and phoenixes, engravings on screens and cabinets often feature scenes from novels such as *Romance of the Three Kingdoms* and *Tales from the Western Chamber*. A simple brass locket, lock-pin or lock-plate can be geometrically intriguing. Even the miniature metal handles for opening drawers can be ornaments in their own right. Restraint in all things is one of Chinese furniture's essential strengths.

Most classic Chinese furniture is fashioned of wood, which in itself has reverential connotations and a historic vibrancy in Chinese cosmology. After all, Chinese call old trees *shen mu*, or God's wood. It is a tribute to the versatile skills of carpenters and artists that their stock-in-trade ranges from oak, elm, cedar, cypress and camphor to pine, teak, walnut, and mahogany.

The cognoscenti favour the prized *huanghuali mu* (yellow flower pear wood), *jichi mu* (phoenix tail or chicken wing wood) and *zitan mu* (dark-purple sandalwood). *Huanghuali* is a yellowish rosewood with fine and subtle markings that was the revered material of Ming Dynasty craftsmen. *Jichi* is so called because of a feather-like grain that enhances the sheen and splendour of the phoenix's plumage. Many Qing Dynasty palace items were made from this rarity.

Marble topped tables in the dining room of
Hong Kong's China Club contribute to the
atmosphere of a restaurant in pre-war Shanghai.

Zitan, an extremely hard rosewood which became largely extinct by the early Qing Dynasty, lends itself to intricate, multi-faceted carving. This is despite the fact that the wood is so dense it sinks in water. In historic times *zitan* and *huanghuali* were as costly as gold and gems. Lately new *zitan* woods to replace those sources in China which had been exhausted have been discovered in Indochina, and Burma.

Many Western connoisseurs have a preference for lacquered or otherwise painted (pigmented) furniture of a more colourful and elaborate design. In recent decades, however, relatively plain hardwood products have found favour with both collectors and habitual users. For variety, post-Qing Dynasty and contemporary furniture makers are increasingly turning to bamboo and rattan, or combinations of disparate materials.

Chinese furniture as we know it did not come into being until the Tang Dynasty (618–907 AD). Before that, Chinese knelt or sat cross-legged on woven mats surrounded by sparse, low-level furnishings. Chairs, stools, tables and the like are believed to have been introduced from neighbouring countries in the wake of the migration of cultures and religions, particularly Buddhism. Art historians tend to the opinion that in terms of style, if not technique, furniture design and carpentry were firmly established during the late years of the Song Dynasty (960–1279).

The Heights of Elegance

Furniture became a true art form of great purity in the Ming Dynasty (1368–1644). The finest Ming examples are celebrations of classic line and understated elegance. Yet chairs, chests and cupboards from this period sometimes exhibit elaborate inlaying and lacquer coatings with engravings and paintings. The canopy beds of the literati were used not only for sleep but for conversation and discussion. Antique Ming furniture is now vastly expensive, much prized by collectors and exhibited world-wide in great museums.

In the Qing Dynasty (1644–1911) there began a shift of taste to more opulent ornamentation. Artisans serving the Emperor Qianlong (1736–1796) added new motifs with subtle Western influences. One of the best examples of the sumptuous Qianlong period is the emperor's rosewood throne, now in the T.T. Tsui Gallery of London's Victoria and Albert Museum. This red-lacquered throne displays minute carvings of cloud-like emblems, flora and fauna, and historical personages in an elaborately sculptured panoply.

It was also during the Ming and Qing periods that carpenters and particularly cabinetmakers perfected ingeniously designed ways of joining wood. Strong, reliable glue had not yet been discovered, so most Ming furniture was bonded by distinctive mortise-and-tenon joints or wooden pegs traversing the intersection. Allowance was made for shrinkage so that the items strengthened in time and in use. Such techniques probably coincided with the prosperous Ming construction of palatial homes in the cities and coastal areas such as Suzhou and Wuxi. The importation of hardwood varieties from Southeast Asian countries encouraged novelty and experimentation in the furniture métier.

Talented carpenters from various regions began to establish distinctive provincial styles. Naturally, the affluent Shanghai-Jiangsu region excelled in opulence and variety of style, but pleasant surprises could be discovered in the hinterland. Shanxi became famous for well-preserved ancient formats as well as slightly garish red and black lacquerware. From Tibet came furniture incorporating Buddhist and other spiritual objects.

The great Ming and Qing designers and craftsmen, like China's great potters, were and have remained unsung heroes. In China, there are no named masters of carpentry comparable to Boulle of France, or Thomas Sheraton and George Heppelwhite of England. Early literature on the subject of furniture is rare. The carpenter's talent and ability did not rate as an art form.

Right: Authentically unpretentious, the Luk Yu 'Eating House' takes its name from scholar and tea connoisseur Luk Yu and values its reputation as Hong Kong's oldest *dim sum* restaurant.

The Chinese tradition of ignoring the achievements of craftsmen who created and made great furniture in the past, continued after the 1949 Communist revolution. During the years of communal chaos between 1966 and 1976 numberless Ming and Qing screens, tables, chests and chairs were either destroyed or burned for fuel. Except for a traditionally negligible minority of intellectuals, household furnishings did not enter the category of art. Not until as late as the 1980s was that age-old trend reversed.

The Custodial Role of Museums

Today the most accessible locations for the appreciation of classic Chinese furniture are the world's great museums. The Victoria and Albert in London comes to mind as does the Museum of Classic Chinese Furniture in Renaissance, California and the Metropolitan Museum of Art, New York. In China itself, as a consequence of traditional attitudes towards furniture and later thoughtless depredations, there is only a limited amount of great classical furniture available to be

viewed. In the Forbidden City – The Great Within – or *Tai Nei* as it used to be termed, is a minimal display of furniture. More examples are available in the great houses of the past in the provinces, for example at Suzhou. In Taiwan, in the well-known Lin residence at Taichuang and in the Cheng residence at Hsinchu, furniture of the traditional Fujian provincial style has been preserved in pristine condition. Sadly little else in China has survived the centuries.

Chinese furniture first found international status through the activities of Western scholars, connoisseurs, collectors and plunderers. In the destruction of the Summer Palace and Yuanmingyuan near Beijing in 1860, virtually the entire furnishings of the palaces were looted by the marauding armies of the Western powers. It is in very large part these items and later loot from another Western raid in 1900 to suppress the Boxer Rebellion, that form the core of the Chinese collections in Western museums today. The 1930s traveller Peter Fleming in his book *The Siege of Peking* commented: "Looting went on squalidly for months, with each nationality blaming some other for setting a bad example and claiming that its own hands were clean".

As a result, by the 1930s and 1940s the collection and study of Ming and Qing furniture had spawned a body of Western experts. European, and increasingly Japanese dealers were in Beijing, Tianjin and Shanghai, eagerly tracking down furniture and purchasing from households which had connections to the Qing Dynasty and its court circles. Yet another source was missionary, diplomatic and expatriate families who far-sightedly had begun accumulating furniture in the early years of the 20th century; much of this, after the Communist revolution, came with them to Hong Kong and so onward to the West.

By the late 1970s Chinese furniture began to be accorded the scholarly attention and status that had long been lavished on Chinese ceramics and painting. And two decades later in the 1990s, the prices of quality Chinese furniture began to set records at Sotheby's and Christie's.

A sound horseshoe back armchair of Ming vintage could command as much as US$100,000. A *zitan* long table with intricate flower carving was sold for more than US$350,000.

The question was then asked: are these prices sustainable? The answer appears to be probably in the affirmative. One reason is the quite limited numbers of fine examples likely to come on the market. The other potent reason relates to the intention of *nouveau riche* Chinese mainland collectors who readily will fly to New York or London to attend auctions when truly fine items of exquisite furniture become available.

There is one salient difference in the study of Chinese classic furniture that separates it from the study of Chinese paintings and ceramics. Authentication is often problematic. Despite the recent tightening-up of customs supervision on the Chinese side, fine furniture still emerges. What muddies the picture somewhat is the reconstruction of whole pieces from parts of several items, some of which may be genuine Ming or Qing, or perhaps not.

Today there are many factories in Qingdao, Panyu and Guangdong capable of reproducing commendable look-alikes for increasingly interested affluent Chinese patrons who aspire to the status of possessing what to them represents Ming or Qing furniture.

To meet the increasing interest in Chinese furniture of this comparatively recent range of collectors, connoisseurs and the uninitiated enthusiast, articles in scholarly and semi-scholarly journals appear with mounting frequency and books are published by spirited amateurs, knowledgeable furniture dealers and dedicated scholars.

Left: Overlooked by a Qing Dynasty screen inset with glass panels depicting the four seasons, a formal trestle desk displays the scholar's 'four treasures': brushes, ink stick, slab and paper.

家具

 Ornately carved, two-door
scroll cabinet, lacquered.
Elm wood. Suzhou. 19th century.

 Two-door, square-legged cabinet with curvilinear
apron. Doors of openwork carving backed by cane
panels. *Yang* wood. Hebei Province. 19th century.

SHANXI PROVINCE

Shanxi's name literally means 'mountains west', which refers to the province's location west of the Taihang Mountains. It borders Hebei to the east, Henan to the south, Shaanxi to the west, and Inner Mongolia to the north. The Great Wall of China forms most of the province's northern border with Inner Mongolia. Shanxi has a continental monsoon climate and is rather arid.

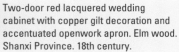
Two-door red lacquered wedding cabinet with copper gilt decoration and accentuated openwork apron. Elm wood. Shanxi Province. 18th century.

Lavishly decorated Chinese export *'bonheur du jour'* writing desk comprising three sections: a two-door cabinet with drawers, a writing slope, and a drawer resting on a stand with cabriole legs that end in ball and claw feet. Qing Dynasty. Circa 1840.

Right: Rendering of gilt lacquer detail from the obverse side of the desk depicting Mandarin courtiers in a rural setting.

 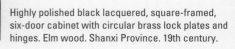 Highly polished black lacquered, square-framed, six-door cabinet with circular brass lock plates and hinges. Elm wood. Shanxi Province. 19th century.

 Square-framed black lacquered cabinet with yellow bronze lock plate. Elm wood. Shanxi Province. Late 18th century.

 A pair of lacquered cabinets, each with two doors, an upper display shelf and a metal lock plate. *Ju* wood. Shanxi Province. Late 18th century.

 Tall two-door tapered cabinet with cedar doorframes backed by rattan matting panels. Beijing, Hebei Province. Contemporary.

 One of a pair of elegantly tapered, round cornered cabinets of polished *Huanghuali* wood. Recessed floating panel doors with hinges of wood. Beijing, Hebei Province. 17th century.

 A beautifully proportioned two-segmented cabinet with a three-drawer shelf between two hump back stretchers. *Longyan* wood. Fujian Province. 19th century.

Left: Red lacquered wedding cabinet with large circular lock plate. The basket-shaped openers represent abundance. Elm wood. Shanghai, Jiangsu Province. 19th century.

Red lacquered wedding cabinet with large circular lock plate. Northern elm wood. Ningbo. 19th century.

Black and red lacquered cabinet, decorated with landscape motifs. Elm wood. Shanxi Province. 19th century.

Two-door, two-drawer, black and red lacquered cabinet, decorated with landscape motifs. Elm wood. Shanxi Province. 19th century.

HEBEI PROVINCE

Hebei Province, with its impressive capital city Shijiazhuang, has a long and proud history, which can be traced back to the Spring and Autumn Period (770 BC–476 BC). It surrounds China's capital, Beijing, and the municipality of Tianjin. It borders Inner Mongolia to the north, Shanxi to the west and Henan to the south. The Great Wall of China cuts through northern Hebei from east to west.

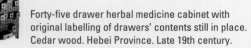

Forty-five drawer herbal medicine cabinet with original labelling of drawers' contents still in place. Cedar wood. Hebei Province. Late 19th century.

 Tapered two-door, red lacquered cabinet with beaded apron. Southern elm wood. Zhejiang Province. Late 18th century.

 An apothecary's cabinet with forty-five drawers. *Ju* wood (Elm wood). Suzhou-Hangzhou. 19th century.

 Two-door, two-drawer, cabinet with door panels of burlwood. Cabinet and frames of doors are lacquered in black. *Ju* wood. Hebei Province. 18th century.

 Gently tapered, two-door book or scroll cabinet on hoof foot legs. Chicken wing wood. Beijing, Hebei Province. 19th century.

 Two-door square shaped scroll cabinet with white bronze *Bai-tong* hinges and locket. Blackwood. Northern China. 19th century.

Right: Detail of circular lock plate of black lacquered cabinet. Elm wood, Shanxi Province. 19th century.

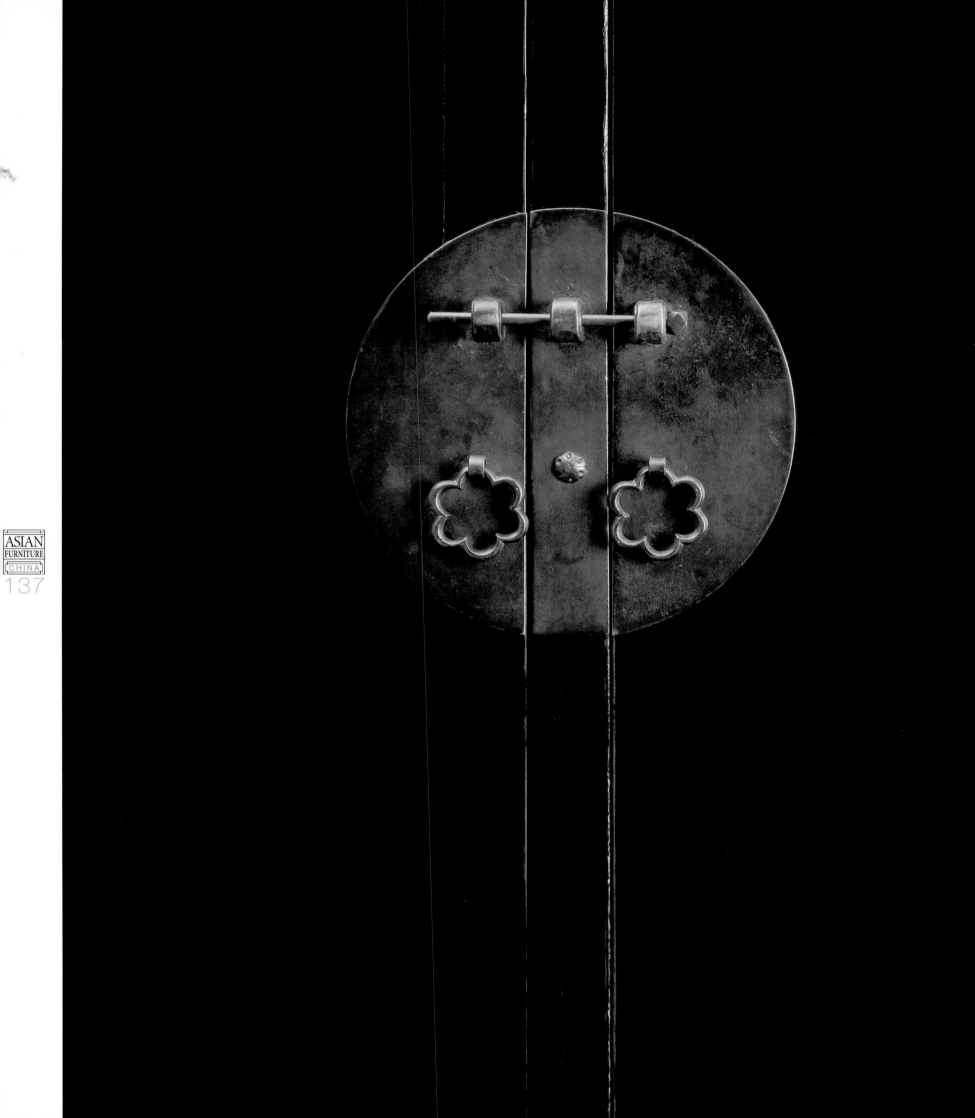

Wardrobe with carved doors featuring vase and floral motifs. Bronze lock plate with vase motif latch. *Huanghuali* wood. Fujian Province. 19th century.

Book or scroll cabinet. *Jichi Mu* (Chicken wing wood). Guangdong Province. Contemporary.

Two-door, two-drawer cabriole legged cabinet with circular lock plate of bronze. Walnut. Shanxi Province. Contemporary.

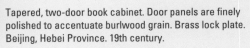
Tapered, two-door book cabinet. Door panels are finely
polished to accentuate burlwood grain. Brass lock plate.
Beijing, Hebei Province. 19th century.

Cabinet with white bronze hinges and
locket. *Huanghuali* veneer on elm wood.
Beijing, Hebei Province. 19th century.

Classic square two-door cabinet with inlaid
yellow bronze hinges. *Huanghuali*. Shanghai,
Jiangsu Province. 19th century.

 Scroll cabinet with separate upper and lower portions. Lower segment has removable front panel. Cedar wood. Anhui Province. 19th century.

 Slatted book cabinet with rodded doors and side panels to provide ventilation. Cedar wood. Shanxi Province. 18th century.

 Red lacquered, square-cornered cabinet, decorated in gold leaf with hand painted motifs of landscapes, pomegranates and butterflies (emblematic of abundance, fertility and joy). Elm wood, Shanxi Province. 19th century.

 Two-door cabinet of red lacquered (auspicious colour of joy and happiness), decorated with golden lotus and butterfly motifs representing purity and joy. Elm wood. Shanxi Province. 18th century.

 Red lacquered, two-door cabinet with painted decorations in gold leaf. Bronze lock panel with latch. Elm wood. Shanxi Province. 18th century.

Extended table of elegant proportions with two-panel surface set in wide frame. The long sides of the carved and shaped apron (left) feature a beaded edge in high relief. Legs terminate in 'garlic head' feet. *Huanghuali*. Shanghai, Jiangsu Province. 16th–17th century.

A recessed-leg lute table with single burlwood top panel set into a *Huanghuali* frame. The legs, which are joined by twin side stretchers, end in metal sabots. Northern China. 17th century.

Small wing table with recessed legs connected by twin side stretchers. Cypress (Baimu). Beijing, Hebei Province. Contemporary.

A rare waistless painting table of *Huanghuali* and nanmuburl associated with the Chinese literati. Splayed round-section legs are joined to the underside of the table by a curved arm brace. Northern China. 16th–17th century.

JIANGSU PROVINCE

Jiangsu Province is located in East China and adjoins Shanghai on the east, Zhejiang Province on the south, Anhui Province on the west and Shandong Province on the north. The provincial capital is Nanjing. Forest resources include bamboo, China fir and pine on the Yi Li hilly land, with yellow and sandalwoods commercially harvested in the Laoshan Forest.

Lacquered three-drawer desk, with latched middle drawer. Apron supported by square arm braces. Elm wood. Shanghai, Jiangsu Province. Contemporary.

Four-drawer writing desk with cracked-ice pattern footrest. *Huanghuali* wood. Beijing, Hebei Province. 20th century.

Lacquered, six-drawer desk with writing surface of rattan, resting on two free-standing supports with stretchers enclosing latticed shelf. Hardwood. Jiangsu Province. Contemporary.

Three-part scholar's desk with four drawers, upper section supported by two-sided pedestals each with one drawer and stretchers enclosing a latticed shelf. Shanghai. Contemporary.

Doctor's travelling desk, with single-board floating panel-top resting on two, two-drawer pedestals. Blackwood. Shanghai. 19th century.

Painting table with single-plank top and upturned ends above a plain apron. Protruding foot stretchers feature inserts with decorative carving. Rosewood. Jiangsu Province. Reproduction.

Detail of altar coffer with deep
relief carving and hanging spandrel.
Shanxi Province. 18th century.

Elaborately embellished side table with framed top plank. Legs are joined at the front and sides by a double stretcher. *Yu* wood. Shanxi Province. Qing Dynasty.

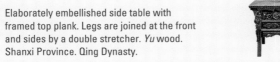

Altar coffer with deep relief carving. Top plank framed by elm wood. Two lower drawers conceal secret compartment. Shanxi Province. 18th century.

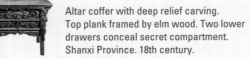

Trestle-table stand with carved lower panels. The upper display area is of symmetrical composition. *Huanghuali* wood. Shanxi Province. 17th century.

 Horseshoe backed armchair with seat of soft matting. The armrest is comprised of three curved segments. The goose-neck struts fitted to both sides are decorative but also provide armrest support. The S-shaped back-splat is free of decoration. Blackwood. Hebei Province. 19th century.

 Southern official hat-style armchair with S-curved back splat. The seat of soft matting is spacious, the overall structure transparent. Stretchers join all four legs. Blackwood. Hebei Province. 19th century.

 A pair of horseshoe armchairs each of four-corner legs supporting a board seat covered by woven rattan, the legs rising through the seat frame to support the horseshoe top rail with side goose-neck struts and from which a backrest of three open-work panels descends to the seat. *Nanmu* and black lacquer. Shanxi Province. 19th century.

 Horseshoe armchair in pre-restoration condition. Relief carved *Ling-zhi* and dragon-cloud motifs on a shaped backrest descending from top rail supported by extended front and back legs and a pair of goose-neck struts. Rectangular seat frame complemented by front apron and hanging spandrels. *Nanmu.* Shandong Province. Late 18th century.

 Southern official's hat-style armchair with openwork carved back splat. The seat board is inset in a rectangular frame. The humpback fore stretcher is well shaped and secured to the vertical struts. Elm wood. Hebei Province. 19th century.

 Southern official's hat style armchair with an elaborately carved openwork back panel and a pair of front aprons. The front and sides are complemented by aprons and hanging spandrels. The footrest apron has survived intact. Elm wood. Zhejiang Province. 19th century.

 A pair of Rose (Wenyi) chairs with an opaque brown lacquer finish. Each has a straight top rail that continues through the rounded corners to the back post. The straight open backs are framed on three sides by inset beaded borders and aprons. Stretchers join the legs. Cedar wood. Hebei Province. 19th century.

Left: A *ruyi*-shaped cartouche detail
framing an auspicious motif of a
mythical lion, from the back splat of
a yoke-back armchair.

A pair of northern official's hat style armchairs with well-matched splats.
The rounded official's hat top rails with swept-back ends are supported on round
S-shaped corner posts. Footrests and stepped stretchers feature curvilinear
aprons carved with leafy tendrils. *Huanghuali*. Hebei Province. 17th century.

Three-tiered two-drawer kitchen cabinet of bamboo. The upper enclosed section used for utensils and the lower ventilated compartment for livestock. Zhejiang Province. Contemporary.

Slender bamboo two-door clothing cupboard, topped by back and side lattice balustrade. Zhejiang Province. Contemporary.

Kitchen cabinet with three storage compartments decorated with folk medallions. Right: Clasp is fish-shaped (symbol of abundance and conjugal bliss). Zhejiang Province. Contemporary.

ZHEJIANG PROVINCE

Zhejiang Province is located on the East China Sea. The capital is Hangzhou. Zhejiang is one of China's most affluent and densely populated provinces. It is mountainous, with only a few passes to the heavily indented coast, chiefly at Ningbo and Wenzhou. Over one third of the area is forested; with pine and bamboo predominating. Most of Zhejiang has a damp climate, with a long, frost-free period and high summer temperatures.

A three-sided asymmetrical and collapsible display cabinet. Lattice design, with lower humped stretcher and struts. Bamboo. Taiwan. Contemporary.

A sturdy four-door kitchen cabinet with curvilinear apron of tortoiseshell bamboo. Taiwan. Contemporary.

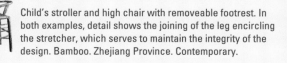 Child's stroller and high chair with removeable footrest. In both examples, detail shows the joining of the leg encircling the stretcher, which serves to maintain the integrity of the design. Bamboo. Zhejiang Province. Contemporary.

 A pair of folk chairs of different size and design. Village furniture, designed and perfected over time, is well engineered and ideally suited to its purpose. Bamboo. Zhejiang Province. Contemporary.

 A reclining chair with sweeping armrests. Backrest and seat are of broad bamboo slats, with X-shaped front stretcher. Zhejiang Province. Contemporary.

Four-poster canopy bed of lofty proportions. The soft matted sleeping platform is enclosed at the back and sides by a rail and lattice. The canopy is decorated with an upper stretcher that encloses openwork-floating panels. An additional humpback stretcher to accommodate a mosquito or privacy net is attached below the canopy. *Longyan* wood. Hebei Province. 18th century.

Six-poster canopy bed, with back and side carved openwork railings in a dragon tendril motif. A footrest and concave rattan pillow are displayed on the soft cane sleeping platform. Ironwood. Northern China. Qing Dynasty.

FUJIAN PROVINCE

Fujian Province is located in China's southeastern hilly area; mountains and hills make up the vast majority of the province, which has a subtropical climate with warm winters. Fujian's coastline is long and intricate, with numerous offshore islands. Fujian is endowed with rich forest resources and mineral deposits. Key industrial output comprises electronics and light industrial products, and in the coastal areas, raw materials and timber.

A plain and geometric four-poster canopy bed of northern design. Lower railings contain paired struts between horizontal rails. Sleeping platform is of woven cane. Cedar wood. Beijing, Hebei Province. 19th century.

Right: A southern-style four-poster canopy bed with deep relief carved floating panels framed between the canopy's upper rails. Enclosed back and side rails feature openwork. Planked sleeping platform above solid outward inclined cabriole feet. Fujian Province. Late 18th century.

Forced high above its surrounding topography by prehistoric upheavals, when the embryonic continents drifted apart and India collided with Asia, Tibet's elevated prominence on the Earth's crust could almost be mistaken for an umbilicus that once connected our planet with the cosmos. So remote and inward-looking is this landlocked Buddhist heartland – whose average altitude is 13,000 feet above sea level – that less than a century has passed since it was first properly mapped. Forty years of Chinese occupation have changed its population profile. Today 6 million Tibetans are outnumbered by 7.5 million Chinese.

The Tibetan tradition of crafting furniture can be traced to the tenth century, when monastic Buddhism experienced its renaissance.

Impatient for that promised paradise in the afterlife, mankind has always needed to believe there is another and better place, a heaven on earth, whether it lies in greener pastures over the hill, at the end of a rainbow or in unexplored lands that will reward the intrepid with their El Dorado.

The thought that, in this world, things might never actually get any better, is unacceptable to some; like being denied any hope of ever winning the lottery or the football pools. To lead us on, we yearn for the metaphysical carrot dangling at the end of that metaphorical stick.

In the age of exploration, the New World was the beacon that lured the hopeful. Later, after Captain Cook penetrated the Tropic of Capricorn and discovered Tahiti, the South Seas sang their siren call. Followed by California and the Gold Rush.

But the gold ran out, the natives turned restless, the fevered dream gave way to fevered blood and disillusionment. Perhaps there was no such place as El Dorado after all.

And then, late in our recent history, came Tibet, remote, isolated, almost inaccessible, and the dream began again; a dream that has never entirely left us, despite all that has happened since. We cling to the idea of Tibet because we associate it with our last ideal of an alternative state of existence, and because we have no other notional "lost world" to spur us on. If not there, beyond the highest mountain range in the world, where else?

Most of us have never been there, but we can visualise, in our mind's eye, hidden valleys overlooked by high, eyrie-ledged monasteries, where deep bells toll and russet-robed, shaven headed monks twirl prayer wheels, solemnly murmuring endless repetitions of *"Om Mani Padme Hum"*.

We forget these monks are warmed by yak-dung fires and lit by yak-butter lamps; that they eat yak meat and yak blood, butter, cheese, and yoghurt; use yaks for transport and weave clothing, blankets and shelters out of yak hair. Shaggy, smelly and unromantic as it may be, the yak is the pivot around which the Tibetan lifestyle revolves. And even Shangri-La has to have its practical, staple necessities.

Searching for Conway, in the Epilogue to James Hilton's novel *Lost Horizon*, Rutherford describes how he met an American traveller who had tried to cross "the least-explored range in the world". "I asked him what he knew about Tibetan lamaseries – he'd been in the country several times – and he gave me just the usual accounts that one can read in all the books. They weren't beautiful places, he assured me, and the monks in them were generally corrupt and dirty. 'Do they live long?' I asked, and he said, yes, they often did, if they didn't die of some filthy disease".

It was Hilton who coined the name "Shangri-La". In a letter dated 24th February 1944 he explains "Eleven years ago, walking late at night near St. Paul's Cathedral, London, I tried to think of a suitable name for a place in a novel I was then writing. It was to be a place of beauty and peace and presently the name came to me: SHANGRI-LA".

Although he never visited Tibet himself, Hilton may have been subconsciously influenced by another name and another traveller. *Shambhala* was the word for the sublime paradise derived from Tibet's pre-Buddhist religion of Bon, which preceded even Hinduism and Jainism in that region.

Russian-born Nicholas 'Yuri' Roerich (1874–1947) was besotted with the idea of *Shambhala* and in 1923 took his family on a five-year pilgrimage around India, Central Asia and Tibet. A lama told Roerich "You Westerners know nothing about *Shambhala*. The secrets of *Shambhala* are well guarded".

To us it seems that many of the secrets of Tibet itself remain well guarded.

Previous page: The ritual rotation of a Buddhist prayer wheel by a devotee at the Potala Palace, Lhasa. Opposite page: (Upper) The Lhasa valley viewed from an upper elevation of the Potala Palace. (Lower left) A finely painted palace door god. (Lower right) Musicians perform during a Buddhist prayer meeting, Shigatse city.

Tibetan Furniture:
Expressions of the Buddhist Faith

Anna Hestler

Hidden behind the Himalayas, in the Land of the Snows, there was once a kingdom where life was lived according to an age-old system of esoteric beliefs. It was ruled by a god-king, the Dalai Lama, and peopled by tonsured monks who spent their days in prayerful contemplation, far removed from the harsh realities of the world. So alluring was this mysterious kingdom that it drew travellers and adventurers from the far-flung corners of the earth. Then tragedy struck. The kingdom was invaded by its neighbours, and the Dalai Lama was forced to seek refuge in another land. But he carried the spirit of his people with him, and to this day he continues to touch hearts and minds across the globe with their story. That story begins in Lhasa with the birth of a Buddhist civilisation whose spiritual philosophy remains a source of inspiration for people throughout the world.

But Buddhist civilisation took root in a much earlier legend that, in common with the primordial myths of most other races, traced the origins of the Tibetan people to a fabulous encounter between pre-human beings. Tibetan mythology relates a curiously simian ancestry that vastly predated Charles Darwin's own explorations of evolution, as expounded in his *Origin of the Species*. In the Tibetan account, their homeland (originally known to them as Bod) arose from the ocean, geologically speaking about forty million years ago, when India collided with Eurasia and formed the Himalayas. There are said to have been two inhabitants of the region, a monkey that preternaturally embodied Chenresig, the Buddha of Compassion, and a lustful ogress. Pitying the lonely ogress, Chenresig's anthropoid progenitor procreated with her, fathering the Tibetan race. This genesis is said to account for the dual nature of the race and to establish Chenresig's preeminent place in the hearts of the Tibetan people.

Lhasa arrived on the historical scene in the seventh century when Songsten Gampo – the fifth in a line of divine kings whom the Tibetans believe were lowered to earth on heavenly cords suspended from the sky – proclaimed it the capital of the Yarlung Dynasty. In the two centuries that followed, Tibet's travelling armies carved out an empire that stretched from the plains of India and the mountains of Nepal to the frontiers of China. An astute leader, King Songsten formed political alliances by marrying Princess Wencheng of China and Princess Bhrikuti from Nepal, both devout Buddhists. It was through their influence that Buddhism gained a foothold in Tibet.

Using their feminine wiles, Songsten's queens converted their husband to their faith and convinced him to introduce it into 'savage' Tibet. The king became a zealous patron of Buddhism, allocating much of his wealth to its endowment throughout his dominion. He built the first temples – the Ramoche and the Jokhang – to house sacred statues brought by his wives as part of their dowries. With its gentle message of compassion, Buddhism had a calming effect on the warlike Tibetans and their relations with their neighbours became more peaceful. King Songsten invited Indian sages to Tibet and sent an emissary to Kashmir to devise a script for the Tibetan language, which was then used to translate the canonical texts from Sanskrit.

Enthusiasm for Buddhism continued to grow for two centuries after King Songsten's death. When Trisong Detson (c. 740–798) ascended the throne, he pronounced it the state religion and founded the Samye Monastery, the first institution to train Tibetan monks. Samye was established in 775, when the Tibetan sangha began with the initiation of seven of these monks. Still, the introduction of the Buddhist religion was no simple matter and it encountered both divine and earthly resistance. According to legend, an Indian mystic named Padmasambhava, known to Tibetans as Guru Rinpoche, had to be summoned to suppress the local gods, who had unleashed thunderbolts and hailstorms to drive all Buddhists out of Tibet. The story goes that Padmasambhava meditated on a diagram of the five celestial Buddhas for seven days, compelling the gods to become protectors of the *dharma*, the Buddha's teachings.

Right: With devotion in their hearts, pilgrims worship the Buddha on hands and knees in the Jokhang – the spiritual heart of Lhasa.

The followers of the indigenous religion, Bon, whose rituals included human sacrifice and the exorcism of demons, resented the new religion. The court divided into pro- and anti-Buddhist factions, which became embroiled in a series of plots and assassinations. When Langdharma assumed power (c. 836), he launched an attack on Buddhism – monasteries were ransacked, sacred books burned and monks were forced to disrobe. In 842 King Langdharma was in turn assassinated by a Buddhist monk and the line of Yarlung kings terminated. In the confusion that followed, Tibet entered a 150-year spiritual dark age.

Rescued by Buddhism

By the late tenth century, Buddhism had reawakened the Tibetan mind. Monks sent to India returned with scriptures on the pursuit of enlightenment: liberation from *samsara*, the endless cycle of birth, death and rebirth. The Buddhist philosophy that captured the Tibetan imagination was a development of the Indian Mahayana school known as Tantrism – an esoteric belief system steeped in ritualism. Tantric Buddhists accepted Mahayana teachings which emphasised the role of the *bodhisattva* – one who, through compassion and self-sacrifice,

relinquishes the prospect of becoming a Buddha to work for the enlightenment of all beings – but rejected the notion of 'gradual' enlightenment. They claimed that through studying the tantras – religious texts that detailed esoteric doctrines and practices – one could attain 'rapid' enlightenment. This involved deep meditation on complex images associated with particular deities and recitation of a mantra, the most sacred being the *om mani padme hum* 'Hail! Jewel in the lotus flower' mantra of Chenresig (Avalokiteshvara), the Bodhisattva of Compassion and Tibet's patron deity.

The point of meditation was to relinquish attachment to the ego, thus releasing it from desire and suffering and freeing one to care for others. Achieving such mental transformation required years of training and only those who dedicated their lives to it could hope for salvation. The goal of the lay folk was simply to secure protection and blessings from benevolent deities; and their religious practices were manifested in pious acts such as making offerings, supporting the monasteries and spinning prayer wheels, which were believed to send a stream of prayer skywards with every rotation. By contrast, tantric initiates studied with a lama, or guru, who transmitted the true spirit of the tantras and passed on his power in the form of secret rites and initiations. Eminent lamas were thought to be reincarnations of Buddhas, *bodhisattvas* or other advanced beings.

Because of the esteem in which lamas were held, several charismatic figures gathered followings of disciples and founded their own sects. By the fifteenth century, political authority had passed into the hands of contending religious hegemonies, one of which would eventually rule the whole of Tibet. In 1357, a young novice named Tsong Khapa (1357–1419) left his village in north-eastern Tibet and embarked on a long and perilous journey to Central Tibet, where he studied at all the main Buddhist schools before founding the Gelugpa order at Ganden monastery near Lhasa. At Ganden, Tsong Khapa espoused doctrinal purity and monastic discipline. His monks had to forgo liquor, evening meals and long naps, and devoted their lives to the study of logic, Tibetan art and culture, Sanskrit, medicine and Buddhist philosophy.

By the time of Tsong Khapa's third successor, Sonam Gyatso (1543–88), even the Mongols had come under the spell of Tibet's powerful new order. In 1578, Chief Altan Khan converted to Tibetan Buddhism and bestowed the title of Dalai Lama, or Ocean of Wisdom, on the head of the Gelugpa. Sonam was immediately proclaimed the incarnation of Chenresig, who is believed to have given the earliest Tibetans the magical food that transformed them from monkeys into men. Shortly before his death, Sonam announced that he would be reincarnated in Tibet and gave his followers signs that would enable them to find him, thus perpetuating the succession of leadership through a spiritual lineage.

A Flurry of Construction

With the help of the Mongols, the fifth Dalai Lama (1617–1682) supplanted a rival sect, becoming both the spiritual and temporal leader of a Buddhist theocracy that ruled all of Tibet. In Lhasa work began on the Potala, which would serve as a palace, a monastery and the seat of the new government. A scholar and a mystic, the fifth Dalai Lama became known as the Great Fifth because he ushered in a new era of flourishing religious and artistic achievement, restoring Tibet to a greatness unseen since its dynastic days. The influence of the Gelugpa spread beyond Tibet and the order enjoyed the patronage of the emperors of China's Ming (1344–1644) and Qing (1644–1911) dynasties. It had taken several centuries, but Buddhism now governed all aspects of Tibetan society, at every level. Everything became subordinated to supporting the monasteries, whose practices were thought to promote the spiritual progress of all living things. Inspired by their faith, the Tibetans became increasingly devoted to embellishing these centres of piety with some of their finest creations: decorative and religious furniture.

The Tibetan tradition of crafting religious furniture can be traced to the tenth century when, following a century and a half of persecution, monastic Buddhism experienced a renaissance and sparked a cultural exchange between Tibet and India, the birthplace of Buddhism: Tibetans travelled to India to study, returning with new ideas and votive objects that fired the imagination of local artisans, and the growth in Tibetan

Buddhism attracted Indian artists to Tibet as well. Although inspired by Indian Buddhism, the distinctive style of Tibetan furniture that evolved was the result of a synthesis of cultural influences from neighbouring countries. The Buddhist arts of the Pala and Newar kingdoms of India and Nepal were an important early influence, as were the Buddhist cultures in Khotan and Kashmir. Pali influence is clearly visible in the rich religious iconography and vibrant colours that characterise Tibetan furniture, and the elaborate woodcarving is credited to Newari craftsmen from the Kathmandu Valley.

As China came to play an increasing role in Tibetan affairs, Chinese artistic traditions too were assimilated. Both the Mongols and the Ming emperors Yongle (1403–1424) and Xuande (1426–1435) were patrons of Tibetan Buddhism and the gifts they lavished upon the monasteries brought Chinese artistic styles such as landscape painting, portraiture and foliate patterns to Tibet – having a revolutionary impact on the decoration of Tibetan furniture which continued during the Qing Dynasty (1644–1911). By the sixteenth century, Tibetan furniture-makers had been incorporating and refining a variety of foreign sources for over five hundred years. With the unification of Tibet under the Gelugpa order, a more cohesive style of furniture design that could be readily identified as distinctly Tibetan began to emerge.

The consolidation of religious and secular power under the Gelugpa meant that the monasteries not only performed the religious functions of the state, but also acted as schools, universities and centres of Tibetan culture. They produced art and religious books and performed rituals for the lay community. As Tibet's monasteries grew larger and more sophisticated, they fuelled the demand for more lavishly painted, carved and gilded pieces of religious furniture, taking the craft to its artistic peak. While some pieces were crafted in workshops attached to the monasteries, others were received as donations from devotees and patrons in order to earn merit, or the assurance of a good rebirth in the next life.

An altar with Buddha and *bodhisattva* images reflects the rich pantheon of Tibetan Buddhism.

The furnishings in temples and monasteries were used in both secular and religious contexts. They included built-in cabinets where cooking pots, teacups and blankets were stored, and chests for transporting and storing tribute treasure or the personal belongings of lamas. There were altar cabinets for displaying Buddhist icons, and offering tables destined to hold incense sticks, butter lamps, bowls of water, dishes of grain and sometimes fruit. Among the most widely used items were the *pegam*, a low cabinet for loose-leaf texts and ceremonial implements, and lama tables for conducting *pujas*, or ceremonies. Portable tables with collapsible panels on three sides were used for outdoor religious ceremonies performed by travelling lamas. The *torgam*, or ritual box, stored *tormas* (barley cakes) offered every evening to protector deities such as the fierce-faced Black Mahakala. Another box, the *yangam*, safeguarded turquoise, gold, silver and other valuables, which represented the treasury of a deity and were used for rituals intended to bring good fortune.

Artisans' Guilds

During reign of the fifth Dalai Lama, furniture-making guilds coordinating the efforts of artists and craftsmen were established, with a view to raising the standards of craftsmanship and creating a more cohesive style of Tibetan furniture. Each guild was headed by a Grand Master, who was responsible for overseeing all work relating to the trade and for ensuring a high standard of quality. Belonging to a guild was considered an honour and would-be artisans would request training by visiting the master craftsman on an auspicious day bearing a *kata*, the traditional white silk offering scarf, and a gift of sweet rice. Once admitted to the guild, the apprentice spent three years in the workshop of the master craftsman, who passed on not only technical skills, but also the secrets of the trade concerning proportions, design and structure. At the end of the period, the apprentice was examined and given a particular ranking, the highest being for government service, the second for homes of important officials or lamas and the third for the households of wealthy merchants.

A commission to produce an article of furniture began with a discussion between patron and master craftsman on the use and subject matter of the piece. After a sketch had been approved, production would commence. The first step in crafting a piece of furniture was to find the right tree – ideally one that was a few hundred years old because the older the wood, the more beautiful the grain. Most pieces were fashioned from softwoods such as pine, spruce, fir or cedar, using tools similar to those in Europe: planes, hammers, saws and chisels. The carpenter's most important tool was the curved adze, or *teptsa*, which was used to shape the wood. Unlike his other tools, which he kept in a leather pouch, the carpenter always kept his *teptsa* safely secured in his belt. When cutting the wood into pieces, the carpenter took great care to preserve its 'essence' and to maintain the beauty of its natural wood pattern. Once the wood had been cut, the sections were assembled into a complete piece using glue rather than nails, which were thought to damage the wood. Having finished the basic structure, the piece was then ready for carving.

Woodcarving was carried out only by those craftsmen who had truly mastered this skill, and could produce a variety of detailed designs to perfection. Buddhist and Bon tutelary deities, as well as numerous auspicious symbols formed the core of the woodcarver's decorative canon. Other popular motifs inspired by Chinese and Indian textile designs included scrolling lotus vines, interlocking coins and geometric patterns. Like the carpenter, the woodcarver did his utmost to preserve the essence of the tree and to create a harmony between the form and function of the piece during the process of carving. The most time-consuming and intricately carved pieces were those to be used in religious ceremonies or placed in prominent positions such as in front of altars or thrones. Once the woodcarver had completed his work, he summoned the decorator who would then brighten up the piece with an explosion of colour.

The term 'decorator' was used to distinguish furniture painters from painters of religious *thangka* and mural who were bound by strict canonical rules as to proportions, symbols and colours. On rare occasions, *thangka* painters would be commissioned to work on important pieces of furniture, since they had been specifically trained to paint Buddhist deities. However, the fact that furniture was viewed as a craft rather than religious art allowed more freedom of expression in furniture decorating, although religion was still the artist's main source of inspiration.

The first job of the decorator was to apply several coats of *gesso* (glue mixed with ground chalk and lime) and then polish the piece to create an even surface for painting. Following this, an outline of the decorative design would be drawn on a sheet of paper and perforated with tiny holes so that it could be transferred to the surface of the wood by dusting black powder over the paper. Since most pieces were made to measure, only the sides that were meant to be visible were decorated. The colours were painted on one at a time beginning with the background and ending with the shading. These were made by grinding minerals: cinnabar (red), malachite (green), azurite (blue), lead (orange) and orpiment (yellow). Sometimes powdered gold from Nepal was added to illuminate the piece or the raised *gesso* technique was used to simulate the scales on dragons and bumpy fruits. Depending on the complexity of the design several painters might be involved in the process, supervised by a master who would contribute the finishing touches.

For the furniture craftsman, all work was a manifestation of his religious beliefs rather than a form of personal expression. Artisans never signed their work and remained anonymous, due to the Buddhist belief in non-attachment to one's ego. Every creation was thought to be an offering for the well-being of all living things and a means of accumulating merit. Pieces to be used in a religious context were particularly important because their beauty was thought to strengthen the faith of all who saw them. Before crafting such a piece, the artisan would meditate in order to infuse the object with spiritual energy. Once the work began, it was carried out unhurriedly and with devotion.

Education through Iconography

The decoration of the furniture was particularly important and the designs varied, since they functioned at different levels of society. In a country where the majority were farmers and nomads, iconography served as a powerful educational tool,

helping the illiterate understand and experience the Buddha's teachings. Many decorative motifs were layered with spiritual meaning not always apparent to the unenlightened. However, viewing the piece on a daily basis was thought to makes one's soul more receptive to the Buddha's wisdom. Non-religious symbols and motifs that reinforced auspicious outcomes, such as luck, happiness and a long life, were also popular among the laity. Many, such as landscapes, dragons and the characters for happiness and longevity were borrowed from the Chinese and then adapted to suit Tibetan aesthetic preferences.

For the elite monastic community, religious images on furniture served to protect Buddhism, the Dalai Lama and Tibet, and as a visual focus for ceremonies. Portraits of Buddhas, *bodhisattvas*, protector deities and revered historical figures were especially potent images because they personified the ultimate levels of wisdom and compassion. Portraits of the Buddha were generally grouped into three categories: fables about his former lives, known as *Jataka Tales*, episodes in the life of the historical Buddha, Shakyamuni; and images of celestial Buddhas who were believed to reside in the heavenly realms. Crowned or jewelled *bodhisattva* figures representing particular spiritual values were often painted on either side of a large seated Buddha. Protector deities were usually depicted in ferocious forms with numerous adornments, symbolising their ability to defend the *dharma*. The most popular guardian depicted on Tibetan furniture was Black Mahakala, whose image was derived from the angry form of the Hindu god Shiva. But not all protector gods featured on Tibetan furniture were horrific representations. Philosophers, teachers and kings who propagated the Buddhist faith constituted a second category of *dharma* protectors and were generally portrayed as exotic-looking monks.

Other furniture designs featured auspicious symbols such as representations of the Three Jewels of Buddhism – the Buddha, the *dharma* and the monastic community. Pieces with such designs were used in ceremonies that marked an initiate's commitment to pursuing the path of enlightenment prescribed by the Buddha. The Eight Auspicious Symbols associated with the Buddha's enlightenment – the wheel of the *dharma*, the endless knot, the golden treasure vase, the parasol,

Restoration work in a small rural monastery attests to the Tibetan people's will and determination to preserve their faith.

the victory banner, the white conch, the golden fishes and the lotus – functioned as visual references to the teaching of the Buddha and as protective motifs. Birds and animals such as the snow lion – protector of the Dalai Lama and Tibet – were also regularly used motifs. Sometimes snow lions were painted amidst clouds above the mountains, an allusion to Buddhism leaping over the Himalayas, like a snow lion, to get from India to Tibet.

Designs created as aids to meditation were the most complex, since their purpose was to heighten spiritual experience and transport the tantric adept to an altered state of consciousness.

Images associated with tantric practices included tigers, skeletons, skulls and meditation deities, which allowed one to go deep into the unconscious mind to clear away mental obstacles that stood in the way of enlightenment. Intricate mandala diagrams representing the sacred universe of a celestial being helped the devotee to envision himself in the divine world so that he could explore enlightening possibilities. Within the mandala, the central deity was usually surrounded by a series of concentric circles containing groups of deities such as guardians or dancing goddesses, which represented different forms of consciousness. The *dorje* (thunderbolt) motif was a reference to the practice of compassion, while the bell signified wisdom and emptiness. These elaborate tantric designs were the ultimate creative expression of the Tibetan spirit and religious beliefs.

Genuine antique furniture from Tibet remains something of a rarity, so that collectors should bear certain caveats in mind when trying to determine an item's authenticity. They should remember that, except for the wealthy, Tibetans used very little furniture in their homes, and their population had always historically remained somewhat small, so that not much furniture was ever made. Most of their furniture was found in monasteries, many of which, along with their contents, were destroyed in 1959 when the Chinese occupied Tibet and the Dalai Lama was forced into exile, or in the turmoil of China's Cultural Revolution (1966–76). As the supply of original, untouched pieces from Tibet has gradually dried up, 'recreated' furniture has been appearing on the market in larger and larger numbers.

Recreated Furniture

The biggest issue is the repainting of furniture. This can run from minor retouching of a worn paint surface to the repainting of an entire piece with new decoration. Besides the problem of repainted furniture, reworking of originals has included the creation of new pieces out of what can be salvaged from the old: refitting a cabinet with doors which may have been salvaged from another cabinet, cutting down a damaged large piece to make a smaller one; marrying parts of a damaged pair to make a single, and other equally 'creative' measures.

The antique value of such pieces is only a fraction of what could have been fetched by the originals, so that reworked furniture should be labelled accordingly, which is not always the case. Recently the situation has deteriorated further. Numerous buyers have discovered that pieces represented to them as 'all original', or only 'retouched', are actually brand new, entirely repainted, or radically 'enhanced' to make them more sellable. This has been the case with cabinets, tables, storage boxes, and shrine cabinets. Prospective purchasers are warned to be especially cautious when considering a piece offered through an on-line auction or directly from a warehouse. Most are repainted, and have even been claimed as 'non-retouched' when sporting a type of decoration unlike that of any genuine Tibetan cabinet ever made.

Collectors seeking authentic Tibetan furniture should be suspicious of any piece with a decorated top. Of the countless cabinets and storage boxes that have passed through reputable galleries, only a handful of boxes had painted tops, and cabinet tops, if painted at all, were only painted with one colour, usually red. Only occasional table tops were painted and one should expect great wear and abrasion in all but the rarest examples. As to painted sides, because so many cabinets originated in monasteries, where they were ranged side-by-side, only a few had one or both sides painted. Boxes from the seventeenth century and earlier were more likely to have painted sides, but these remain very expensive because of their beauty and rarity.

Finally, if the paint looks too good to be true, it probably is. Most Tibetan furniture has gone through nearly as hard a time as its owners, and its decoration shows it. If the painting has been freshly embellished, one would expect to see that at least the underlying piece shows traces of wear and tear. Scrapes, indentations and hand chamfering are to be expected. It also helps to keep in mind the decorative motifs of original pieces. Fanciful animals found on many items advertised on-line bear little resemblance to animals as rendered by Tibetan artists. One of the surest exposés of newly painted furniture is in the simple painting style, which displays little care or attention to detail and none of the love and painstaking labour that original artists would have lavished on their works.

Although many of Tibet's artistic treasures were swept away by the Cultural Revolution, there is hope that the spirit of the Tibetan people will continue to express itself through Buddhist art in all its forms. In Dharamsala, the Tibetan community-in-exile is striving to preserve its rich culture. At the Norbulingka Institute, painters and woodcarvers train under the guidance of masters in accordance with the apprenticeship system which prevailed before the Chinese occupation of Tibet in 1959. Aided by their Buddhist faith, Tibetan artists are rediscovering sacred Buddhist art and regaining their own artistic voice. Having survived the ordeal of exile and the loss of their homeland, the Tibetans are determined to preserve the ancient Buddhist traditions which form the core of their artistic and cultural heritage. Their indomitable spirit is inspiring.

ཤིང་ཆས

A pleasing blend of vivid colour and Buddhist symbolism, this 18th century temple chest of light pinewood reflects the artistic spirit of Tibet.

The soft floral pattern on this 19th century household chest, not a traditional Tibetan motif, was probably inspired by textiles imported from Europe or India.

A temple throne, gilded with snow lion images, from which the High Priest would deliver his homilies. The emblems represent the protectors of Tibet, Tibetan Buddhism and the Dalai Lama. Opposite page, detail of the headboard.

With its delicately rendered floral décor, this two-door and three lower drawers cabinet exudes a tranquillity of its own. Because of the harsh climate Tibetans are exposed to, they have a special devotion to flowers which has prevailed from an early age. Each flower has its appropriate and emblematic significance. Late 19th century.

Skilfully crafted in gesso (raised oil paints) the richly textured floral pattern on this storage chest exemplifies the craftsmanship of Tibetan artisans. 18th century.

For centuries, Tibet's artists have drawn inspiration from work in silk and brocade by their Chinese counterparts, translating their impressions into bold, beautiful designs such as those on this six-panelled clothing chest. 18th century.

Gilded, wooden prayer table with open fretwork design of intertwined floral motifs, used for prayer and meditation by eminent lamas. 18th century.

 In old Tibet, the common man stored household items in a yak-skin sling bag, while a man of means stored them in gilded cabinets like this exceptionally finely decorated two-door piece.

 The Wheel of Life, one of the Eight Auspicious Symbols of Buddhism, is depicted here on the centre panel of a bedding storage cabinet. An icon of the Buddha's teaching, the wheel's eight spokes represent the Noble Eightfold Path of Enlightenment. Late 18th century.

 Household storage chest decorated with scenes from Tibetan mythology. On top, a water bowl and vessel used for ritual offerings. 19th century.

A quiet harmony of colours complements the religious symbolism on this monastery cabinet of pinewood: the animal pyramid donates cooperation; the teacher and his disciples represent shared wisdom.

The lotus flowers on this treasured 18th century household cabinet denote purity and compassion, while the white conch shells symbolise the delivery of the Buddha's doctrine.

Raised storage trunk painted with lotus flowers, the wheel of the *dharma* and an offering of fruit. On display, an image of the founder of the Gelug-pa sect, a ritual bell and sceptre and a lama sculpture. Late 17th century.

Left: Finely executed detail of an altar table made of brittle pinewood, elaborately painted with mythical creatures symbolising victory over disharmony.

A four-panelled, square monastery table on which are placed a silver image of the Buddha and a bell, associated with the idea of respect and reverence and rung during rituals or when convening an assembly of monks.

 With its delicately rendered floral décor, this cabinet exudes a tranquillity of its own. Late 19th century.

 Household storage chest with gold-based floral pattern. On display, an image of a deity with silver reflective ornaments on either side to ward off inauspicious influences. 19th century.

 The images of wrathful figures on this altar table may seem at odds with the Buddha's peaceful message; nevertheless they are intended as aids to the devout in their pursuit of understanding. On display, the carved wooden covers of Buddhist scriptures.

Right: Upper panel detailing one of the Eight Auspicious Symbols of Buddhism, the Wheel of the Law, the lower panel features an animal pyramid, denoting cooperation.

A pair of monastery cabinets decorated with phoenix motifs. The phoenix, as the Emperor of all birds, is adorned with everything that is beautiful in the bird kingdom. Legend has it that the phoenix appears in times of peace and prosperity and will not harm any living creature, as the Buddha taught.

In monasteries throughout Tibet the extent of a cabinet's décor suggests its location in a room. Those decorated on three sides (like that shown here) stand proudly in their own space, rather than being sidelined in corners or placed between other pieces.

Treasure chest of fine pinewood, coated in leather, with entwined dragons viewed as auguries of wealth, influence and happiness.

Pinewood monastery chest covered in leather. (See following page.)

Monastery chest. A pair of tigers, whose stripes stand for bravery and ferocity, protect the Three Jewels of Buddhism: The Buddha, his teachings and the sangha, the community of believers.

An 18th century red lacquered
treasure chest on which are
displayed leather-bound bookends
depicting images of the Buddha.

Household storage chest adorned with vividly coloured peonies
in passionate bloom, the emblem of love and affection and a
symbol of feminine beauty. This piece of furniture was displayed
in the foyer of the home for all to behold and admire.

 A portable leather trunk with metal braces and a centrally located lock plate adorned with a wind horse, a mythical animal associated with the swift delivery of messages and blessings. Late 18th century.

 A two-door monastery offering chest. Images of the protector deity, Black Mahakala, surrounded by several heads, symbolise triumph over the darker aspects of the human psyche. 19th century.

 This substantial piece from Lhasa, a sturdy, elegant, cabinet with two drawers and two removable front panels, features a floral motif on lacquer, reflecting Qing Dynasty stylistic influences.

 Images of the protector deity, Black Mahakala, surrounded by severed heads, symbolise triumph over the darker aspects of the human psyche. Two-door, monastery offering chest of red lacquer. Late 17th century.

 Banded with iron slats, this red lacquered, two-door monastery cabinet was used to store temple paraphernalia, such as water bowls, jugs of yak butter, bells and incense sticks. The carrying handles on either side enabled it to be carried from monastery to monastery, accompanying the lama on his travels.

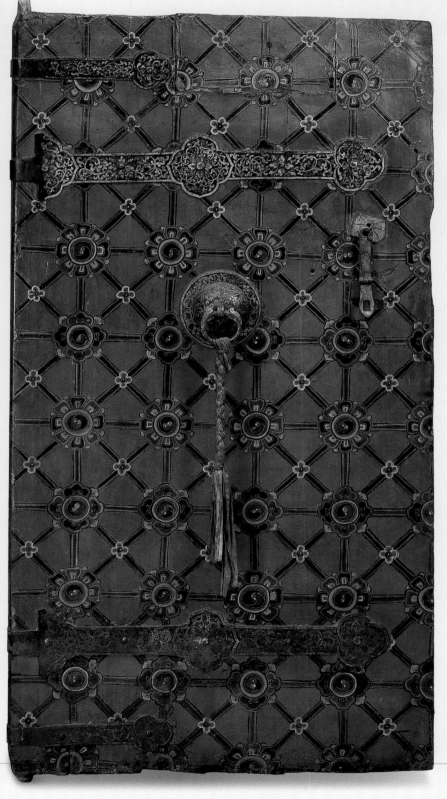

 Lion hides radiate sheer energy and seem barely contained within the restricted space allotted them on this window shutter. Late 19th century.

 Although inspired by Ming Dynasty China, this 17th century monastery door with gilded iron fittings and tasselled door knocker once led to an esoteric world that was unmistakably Tibetan.

 This wooden door serves as a visual metaphor for overcoming destructive emotions, here symbolised by the tiger (anger) and the horse (jealousy).

 Painted door depicting monks of the Gelug-pa sect sounding conch shell trumpets and animals associated with Mahakala, the chief protector of the *dharma*.

 Cartoon-like lion replicas radiate boundless force and seem barely contained within the restrictive framework of these window shutters. Late 19th century.

 A carnival of colour, the menagerie of animals on this cabinet's side panel represent the Buddhist concept of reincarnation. The attention to detail and colour given this piece of furniture merited display in the most prominent position of the house, where it could be admired by all.

Vulnerable to sweeping political as well as climatic changes, the scattered and volcanic Philippine islands straddle the path of the many typhoons spawned in the tempestuous Philippine Sea. Bearing the name of a long-dead Spanish king, the country still nurtures, at its heart, some of the fiery spirit and gravitas of the Spanish conquistadors whose colonial successors held it in thrall from 1565 to 1898. A deep love of music, richly imprinted in the genes of its 88 million people, has been carried around the world by a far-reaching diaspora impelled through force of economic circumstance. Wherever they go, Filipinos take their songs and their sunshine with them.

Fedor Jagor, who travelled the Philippines in the late 19th century, described the archipelago as "a lotus-eating Utopia". "In other countries," he remarked, "with an equally mild climate, and an equally fertile soil, the natives, unless they had reached a higher degree of civilization than that of the Philippine Islanders, would have been ground down by native princes, or ruthlessly plundered and destroyed by foreigners.

"In these isolated islands, so richly endowed by nature, where pressure from above, impulse from within, and every stimulus from the outside are wanting, the satisfaction of a few trifling wants is sufficient for an existence with ample comfort".

Jagor found the Filipino "an interesting study of a type of mankind existing in the easiest natural conditions". Spanish rule in these islands "was always a mild one, not because the laws, which treated the natives like children, were wonderfully gentle, but because the causes did not exist which caused such scandalous cruelties in Spanish America and in the colonies of other nations".

Spaniards who arrived in 1565 to colonise the Philippines as a province of Mexico found the native houses devoid of furniture.

Jagor also found that, though Spanish manners, religion and language were willingly imitated, Filipino respect for their colonial masters was "diminished by the numbers of these uneducated, improvident, and extravagant Spaniards, who, no matter what may have been their position at home, are all determined to play the master in the colony".

This compulsion to assert their superiority was perhaps understandable. Once settled in the Philippines, few Spaniards ever returned to Spain. To do so was forbidden to the priests, and most of the rest had no means of affording the return journey. A considerable portion consisted of subaltern officers, soldiers, sailors, political delinquents and refugees whom the mother-country had expelled. Among them were adventurers lacking both means and desire for the journey back, "for their life in the colony is far pleasanter than that they were forced to lead in Spain".

The Spanish expatriates arrived without the slightest knowledge of the country and without being in the least prepared for a sojourn there. "Many of them are so lazy that they won't take the trouble to learn the language even if they marry a daughter of the soil. Their servants understand Spanish, and clandestinely watch the conversation and the actions, and become acquainted with all the secrets, of their indiscreet masters, to whom the Filipinos remain an enigma which their conceit prevents them attempting to decipher".

Cultural assimilation was a one-way street. Along with everything else they absorbed into their lifestyle, the natives adopted the furniture of their conquerors. Jagor visited several indigenous families and received a friendly reception from all of them. He described houses built of boards and placed upon piles elevated five feet above the ground. Each consisted of a spacious dwelling apartment which opened on one side into a kitchen, and on the other onto an open space, the *azotea*. The floor was composed of slats an inch in width and laid half that distance apart. Chairs, tables, benches, a cupboard, a few small ornaments, a mirror, and some lithographs in frames, composed the furniture of the interior. "The cleanliness of the house and the arrangement of its contents testified to the existence of order and prosperity".

The author sought in vain the distinctly marked national customs he had expected to find in such an isolated part of the world. "Again and again the stranger remarks that everything has been learned and is only a veneer". It was as if Spanish influence had erased all trace of what had been, and ethnic Filipino culture – if not its pre-colonial history – had vanished beyond recall, leaving the country's ethos to begin afresh on a blank page.

Previous page: Cupids adorn a fountain in the gardens of Fort Santiago, the main citadel of Manila, built in 1570. Opposite page: (Upper left) Plaza de la Fuerza in the old Spanish walled city of Intramuros. (Upper right) Memorial to the Philippines national hero José Rizal. (Lower) Interior of the 400-year old San Agustin Church, Manila.

Philippine Colonial Furniture, 1580–1900

Martin I Tinio Jr

Spaniards who arrived in 1565 to colonise the Philippines as a province of Mexico found the native houses devoid of furniture because Filipinos, like most South-east Asians, squatted on the bamboo floors of their homes, stored their clothes in rattan baskets and slept on mats that were rolled up, out of the way during the day. Meals were served on plates spread on the floor, although the ruling classes had their meals presented on footed wooden or brass trays or a *dulang*, a low table similar to those in use by the Japanese and Koreans.

Life initially was difficult in Manila, the capital of the fledgling colony, where the population lived in huts and where food and materials were in short supply. Until 1600, the best that could be said of anyone living in Manila was that 'he eats well'. After a fire completely destroyed the city in 1583, everyone was (legally required) to invest in modest, tile-roofed stone houses with a *sala* or salon, a single bedroom and a balcony. The Chinese carpenters who built these dwellings also provided the chattels – copies of furniture from Mexico or versions of Ming-style furniture – all with traditional Chinese joinery, without the use of nails, for iron was scarce and had to be imported. Since there were no Philippine words for furniture, these items came to be designated by their Spanish names, which are still in use today.

To attract settlers, every Spanish resident of Manila, depending on his status, was assigned cargo space in the galleons that plied the Pacific to and from the New World. Under Spanish rule Manila became an international port and Asia's commercial entrepot. *Intramuros* (Latin for 'within the walls'), the local name for Manila, evolved as Asia's largest European city and the most securely fortified stronghold in the Pacific.

For centuries, some 30,000 traders from Asia and as far away as Madagascar converged on Manila from March to May to trade silks, spices, ivory, porcelain, gems and of course slaves in return for Mexican silver dollars. The goods were then transshipped to Mexico, Panama and Peru. Although banned in 1621, trade with Peru clandestinely continued until 1706. The Asian goods were easily disposed of in America, while European merchandise was purchased as the return cargo. A successful voyage could yield a tenfold profit, but a shipwreck or a vessel's capture by marauding English or Dutch pirates resulted in hard times and financial difficulties that had to be endured until the next successful voyage.

Above: The *sala* or salon was a grand space for gatherings known as *tertulias*. The room with its red and yellow embellishments has the aura of the *bandera española*, the Spanish flag, and is lavishly decorated in the 1880s Philippine style.

Left: The *sala* of Villa Escudero in Tiaong, Quezon Province, features an Egyptian style table with sphinxes carved from *narra* wood supporting a single slab of Carrara marble.

The 17th Century

The 17th century was a saga of shipwrecks, wars against the Dutch for control of Formosa and the Moluccas (now Taiwan, Malaysia and Indonesia), Muslim raids against native settlements throughout the archipelago, revolts by the Chinese, earthquakes and the plague. Despite these calamities craftsmen in the Chinese district of the Parian – outside the walls of Manila – made magnificent cabinets during the early decades of the century. Their ebony frames, embellished with gilded bronze and silver plaques, were inlaid with gold, ivory, tortoiseshell and mother-of-pearl. Spanish, Chinese, Ceylonese and Indian influences were combined with only one objective – to impress any potential customer with the intricate workmanship and precious materials employed! Their furniture created such demand in Mexico and Peru that the Mexicans eventually imitated it, using a great deal of nacre inlay, dubbing them *mueble enconchado*, literally 'shell-inlaid furniture'. Due to calamitous fires, typhoons and the ravages of war, no examples exist in the Philippines, and the few extant pieces available can be found only in museums in Mexico and Peru.

The heyday of the galleon trade resulted in a spate of house construction by Chinese builders who guaranteed completion and deliver of the house within the year, requiring no deposit, thus allowing the owner the luxury to gamble his investment in the galleon trade and finance the entire cost of the commissioned house and its furnishings from the profits earned. Like contemporary houses in Europe and America, the completed mansions were almost void but for a few massive pieces of furniture, designed and constructed to last. Valuable because of its scarcity, until the end of the century, furniture was commonly used as financial security for further loans.

Every household would have a solitary bed, a table and a handful of chairs with ramrod-straight backs, all of *narra* (*Pterocarpus indicus* Willd. forma *indicus*), a medium-hard wood that was commonly exported as ballast in junks trading with China, where it was prized as *huanghuali*. To divide the huge spaces and impede the drafts that Europeans were commonly resentful of, almost every house had a *cancel*, a folding screen of pine, the Chinese varieties painted in vermilion red – for good luck, and decorated with gold leaf, while the Japanese *beobo* (the Hispanic version of '*biobu*', its Japanese name), came in black lacquer ornamented in gold leaf or gold dust.

The bedroom had a Spanish-style 'four-poster', with a headboard of turned wooden balusters and a canopy for the master and his wife – the rest of the family and servants slept on mats on the floor. Since clothes were prized and also costly, the few that a family owned were stored in woven rattan chests, sometimes strengthened by *narra* frames. *Narra* planks, when made into chests, always had *cantoneras*, corner plates, and a hasp of wrought iron, while pine chests from China had copper plates to reinforce their red and gilt surfaces. All who had sailed the Pacific owned a *caja marinera*, a ponderous sea chest with wrought-iron handles and sturdy hasps with monstrous padlocks to safeguard cash and other valuables brought to and from the New World. From the 1780s some houses had an *aparador*, a two-door cupboard with finials on its corners and panelled doors occasionally carved with Chinese or Southeast Asian motifs. Some, like the *aparador de barandillas*, had rows of turned wooden balusters on their doors that allowed air to circulate in order to prevent damp and mildew.

Houses of the time had no designated space for meals, and the dining table was relocated at will. Families in those days had few children, for many newly arrived adventurers tended to marry widows who already had a house and a source of income. A three-foot diameter circular table with a solid top sufficed for a small family, while a three by four feet oblong table was required for a family with more offspring. Rectangular tables always had framed tops and cabriole legs with clawed feet that rested on stretchers for greater stability. Occasionally made of *kamagong* or ebony (*Diospyros discolor* Willd.), a fine, extremely hard and heavy black wood with a reddish-brown tinge, the legs were embellished at the knees with fierce-looking grotesque masks with bulging eyes and tongues protruding in the native and Mexican symbol of welcome. The masks and their floral and foliate motifs, indigenous to the Moluccas, joined the Philippine repertoire of ornamentation with the arrival of 200 Catholic families from Indonesia in 1663 – after the Dutch conquest. These motifs became the rage in Manila

in the 1750s, and can still be found incorporated in Indonesian furniture today.

Officials and businessmen invariably owned a *contador* (Spanish for counter), a portable chest with a hinged fall-front and lockable drawers. It took the form of a writing desk when placed on a table and usually was accompanied by an abacus of mahogany or ivory beads. A *contador* could be made of plain *narra* with corner plates and hasp, or inlaid with bone or *lanite* (*Wrightia pubscens* R. Br. subsp.), a soft, light toned wood. Every literate lady, a rarity in those times, would own a writing desk with sloping lid in red and gilt lacquer from China or Japan, known as an *escribania* or *escritorio*, adorned with her initials, silver corner plates and lock.

Catholic Spaniards naturally had an *urna* or tabernacle containing an image of Christ, the Blessed Virgin or a favourite saint surmounting a *mesa* altar, in the form of a Ming splay-legged side table.

The 18th Century

The Bourbon accession to the Spanish throne in 1700, dramatically transformed the dark, austere impression of Iberian interiors. Under French influence, dining rooms made a more frequent appearance, furniture became lighter and more comfortable, and new innovations were introduced for innumerable purposes. From Seville, Spain's largest and most influential city, the new Rococo style crossed the seas to Mexico and the Philippines where, by mid-century, many Manila houses could be described as luxuriously furnished even by European standards, replete with splendid furniture, paintings and mirrors.

Right: A *Comedor* (dining room) decorated in the *estilo Tampingco* style or early Philippine art nouveau, characterised by profuse floral and leaf motifs.

Houses now had diverse types of beds, including inexpensive rattan examples and plain beds devoid of ornamentation. The best beds were crafted of finely turned ebony, inlaid with bone and then gilded. In rare instances the painted and gilded *tanguile* bed frame had ivory bedposts supporting the canopy.

Prosperous citizens required clothing storage space, so Parian artisans crafted large, eight feet high cabinets, flanked on either side by turned pillars. Some had inside drawers, while others had glazed doors known as *escaparates para guardar ropas*, literally 'glass cabinets for keeping clothes'. Weapons, standard male accoutrements in those unsettled times, stood ever ready for immediate use in a stand known as an *armero*. A Spanish general would have a carved and gilded wooden *armero*, while a lesser officer would have a six feet-wide armrack of *tindalo* (*Afzelia rhomboidea*). The wood was prized in China as *jichi mu*, chicken-wing wood, because its grain resembled the shape of the wing.

Although every house had sundry types of tables, a circular table with a solid three-foot diameter top of ebony or *tindalo* was a staple as centrepiece of every *sala*. Deemed superior, however, were the painted and gilded Cantonese tables in the Chippendale Style with elaborately scalloped aprons and ball-and-claw footed cabriole legs. The use of *tindalo* for cabinetry meant that large *narra* trees for leagues around the metropolis of Manila were exploited, and wood for furniture had to be felled in the surrounding mountains where *tindalo* could still be harvested.

Chairs became available by the score. A general's salon in 1750, would contain a veritable forest of chairs; twenty-four gilded, straight-backed chairs, eighteen ordinary chairs from the Parian, forty-eight stools and chairs embellished with almost a kilogram of beaten silver! Governor General Arandia had a dazzling display of *tindalo* chairs, several with leather seats and backs, including finely crafted oval chairs from Canton, all completely gilded.

Benches or *bancos* had wide, single-plank seats almost thirteen feet long. Plain benches were relegated to the kitchen while those with backrests found their way into the *caida* (literally 'fall'), the landing at the top of the stairs, so-called because ladies were obliged to lift their full skirts as they mounted the stairs and let them 'fall' upon reaching the landing.

Bureaucrats would require a *papelera*, a container with lock and secluded drawers. A large five-foot high *papelera*, known also as a *condesa* (literally 'countess'), came with doors and a stand with cabriole legs. The fashionable red and gold lacquered *papelera de maque* with its stand or matching table also became the rage in contemporary Europe, where they were opulently displayed in palatial homes.

Numerous screens made their appearance in 18th century Manila. From the Parian came screens twelve feet-wide with as many as fourteen to twenty carved and painted panels, as well as *tindalo* dividers and *tanguile* screens of red and gilt lacquer, the latter so skilfully crafted that they were often mistaken for Cantonese imports. Similar Chinese screens, shipped to Europe from the Coromandel Coast of India, became known in the West as Coromandel screens and are known as such even today. In Manila small, profusely carved and gilded Chinese folding screens enjoyed great popularity, as did the Japanese version which found their way to Manila, despite the Philippines' prohibition of trade with foreigners after Japan had expelled all Christians at the end of the 16th century.

The British Invasion

The Seven Years War (1756–1763), between France and Britain drew many European powers into the fray, with Britain laying claim to most Spanish colonies worldwide. The authorities in Madrid, not expecting the conflict to reach the shores of the Philippines, failed to inform Manila of the hostilities and thus, when thirteen British ships with more than 3,000 troops onboard quite unexpectedly sailed into Manila Bay in 1762, the local Spaniards thought the British had come to trade.

Archbishop Rojo, the acting Governor General, declined to surrender to the British despite the fact he had only 550 Spaniards to defend the city. Daily bombardments finally took their toll, and the Archbishop eventually acceded to a ransom

demand in order to spare the city from further damage and looting. A nocturnal escape by Spanish forces just before the invaders entered the City and Spanish guerrilla tactics confined the British to Manila and its environs until 1764, when they finally received word that the Treaty of Paris had ended the conflict the previous year.

The foreign occupation of Manila, the Chinese abandonment of the Parian for fear of being accused of collaboration with the enemy and the British embargo on trade with all Spanish possessions halted economic activity and left a ruined and destitute colony that required a decade to return to any semblance of normalcy. The galleon trade was waning as the increasing cost of Asian merchandise coupled with the dwindling Mexican demand for silk and oriental goods now rendered a mere 50% return per voyage in place of the ten-fold earnings previously. To exacerbate matters, Canton replaced Manila as the centre of Asian trade due to Europe's insatiable demand for tea.

In a twist of fate, the British occupation engendered a European awareness of Philippine agricultural products. When King Carlos III of Spain encouraged trade between the Motherland and its colonies, the Philippines responded by trading directly with all international ports even those as remote as the Cape of Good Hope. Spanish ships that began to sail directly to Manila in 1778, brought with them a demand for abaca (Manila hemp), sugar and indigo, which encouraged Spaniards in the Philippines to engage in agriculture, stimulating the moribund subsistence economy of the provinces. Waking up to this opportunity, local Chinese married native women in order to be allowed to settle and trade in the provinces, where they were able to purchase land. The expansion of these agricultural holdings created a merchant/planter class, the forerunners of the landed gentry that would dominate Philippine society in the century to follow.

A corner of the *sala* (living room) of the Museo De La Salle in Dasmariñas, Cavite Province. Above the piano hangs an oil portrait of Doña Rosario Gonzalez of Pampanga Province.

Commerce with Europe brought with it foreign periodicals filled with illustrations which had a positive influence in the manufacture of Philippine furniture. *Tindalo* beds with turned posts, headboards and caned mattress supports were painted red like their Spanish counterparts. Ebony, previously used only for bedposts, was now incorporated throughout the entire bed. By 1790, beds made entirely of *narra*, were supplied with an accompanying night table with an upper drawer and a lower cabinet door.

Wardrobes, on occasion, had fashionable wire trellis door fronts as in Europe. *Teka* (*Tectona philippinensis* Benth. & Hook f.), Philippine teak, was used for cabinets, but cheap vermilion-painted *tanguile* was preferred. Blue, since Roman times the most desired colour, was fast becoming fashionable, since it derived from indigo which was readily available in the Philippines, being one of the colony's primary exports. Like the contemporary French armoire, the now-obsolete arms rack or *armero* of the 1750s was transformed into a large carved and painted *tindalo* wardrobe, often seven feet tall and almost as wide.

As large, four-foot diameter circular tables became the vogue. Rosewood examples were imported from Canton and also made locally in *molave* (*Vitex geniculata/parviflora*, Bl.), a heavy wood that turned mellow brown with age. Spectacular six feet wide single-plank *tindalo* tops for circular, square and octagonal tables were sawn from the wide buttresses of gigantic trees that grew in ever-distant jungles. Tables with surfaces composed of several planks were invariably camouflaged a bright red to disguise the joints, while legs were entirely gilded. Three or four-sectioned tables that could be joined together became stylish, along with rectangular examples with *narra* central panels and legs slightly less massive than those of the previous century, now decorated with benign masks on their knees.

Affluent households now had scores of chairs, some in the heavy but popular English Chippendale style. Turned *tindalo* chairs with seats and backrests in plain or gilded leather were later made in the Carlos III Style that was contemporaneous with the French Louis XVI Style. The *silla para servicio*, a night

commode with its receptacle, made its debut in the 1780s, the same decade they became popular in Europe. The Chinese bamboo chairs that inspired the revival of the Chinoiserie Style in Regency England also found their way into Philippine *salas*. Carved Chippendale *tindalo* stools were now upholstered in plush velvet, while the Carlos III varieties with turned legs had caned or gilded leather seats. The nascent plantation lifestyle in the 1780s developed the *silla de poltrona*, literally 'a lazy chair'.

Laguna also turned out *canapes* in rattan. The eight feet long *baticuling* examples could seat four people, while the *lanite* settees sometimes had latticed backs in the Chinoiserie Style. Carved Cantonese sofas with caned seats and backrests had their blue-painted frames highlighted with gold leaf, while the *tindalo* Carlos III Style settees had turned legs, oval backrests and caned seats.

The 19th Century

Although the Napoleonic Wars halted trade with Europe, American clipper ships plying the China Trade discovered that Manila hemp, sugar, rum, tobacco and indigo made profitable cargoes. The United States soon became the Philippine's major trading partner, an interchange that left its mark on local furniture. The Duncan Phyfe Style with its American Federal and English Sheraton influences was manifest throughout the first half of the 19th century, the delicately painted designs of the latter locally executed in bone inlay.

Wealth, expressed in lavish hospitality during fiestas, resulted in dining rooms with longer tables that often had *cabeceras*, D-shaped or polygonal sections at each end where the principal guests were seated. Since borrowing tableware for a dinner, even if guests numbered in the hundreds, resulted in loss of pride, several glass-fronted cabinets were required to contain the tableware needed for entertaining. The quality of the tableware was manifested by the name given to the cabinets. The simple *aparador para guardar platos*, literally 'cabinet for keeping plates', became an *aparador de losa*, a 'cabinet for porcelain' when fine porcelain came into use. It was finally called an *aparador de vajilla*, a 'cabinet for a dinner service' when large dinner services were imported from France and Germany. Large-scale entertainment required cabinets for silver and crystal, so the corresponding and matching *aparador de platera* and *aparador de cristaleria*, came into being. A centre table, sometimes of *alintatao* framed in ebony and with four pillars for legs, now took pride of place in the *sala*, while a small, three foot-wide table that held the chocolate service during *merienda* or high tea attested to the leisurely lifestyle of the era.

Writing tables became popular, because businessmen often transacted their affairs in the *entresuelo* or mezzanine of their domiciles and had to provide desks for their office employees. The secretary-bookcase had line-inlay in white *lanite* and ebony, which became popular when Britain went into deep mourning after the death of Lord Nelson in the Battle of Trafalgar in 1805, going so far as to decorate furniture in black. Its adaptation in Philippine furniture underscored the growing presence of British traders who started arriving when the port of Manila was again opened to world trade in 1830.

Chairs and sofas were often inlaid with ebony. The wide-armed *silla frailuna* or 'friar's chair', now known as the *sillon fraile*, very much an emblem of Philippine's furniture, was originally a fixture in the balcony of the parish *convento* or manse which then found its way into private homes.

The restoration of King Fernando VII to the Spanish throne in 1813 reinstated traffic with the Motherland, but the revolt of Mexico finally ended the Galleon Trade, and commerce with Spanish America was resumed only in the 1870s.

From the 1850s imported furniture became fashionable. Cabinets with full-length, mirrored doors were a status symbol of the era. Large mirrors from Spain were so costly that pretentious households had several installed to underscore their affluence. Although *baticuling* wardrobes still appeared painted red or green, those made of mahogany were now varnished to a glossy finish with *almaciga* (copal). Glossy furniture, inspired by French varnish or *vernis Martin*, then became the rage, to the extent that furniture was annually given a shiny new coat of varnish prior to the town fiesta.

Kalantas or Philippine cedar cabinets became modish in the 1860s to contain the European-style woolen clothing required by social lions attempting to emulate the European – despite the sweltering tropical heat.

Dressing tables that had became fashionable in European bedrooms in the 1860s started to appear in Manila homes as a *lavador* or washstand, a simply decorated stand for a basin with a lower shelf for a pitcher. Eventually it evolved into a larger *narra* version with shelves to contain toiletries and other sartorial paraphernalia and then became the *lavador con tocador*, which combined the dresser and washstand. In influential households the master and mistress had their individual dressing table, whose low *narra* frame was surmounted by a gilded and tilting mirrors. Some gentry allowed themselves a separate diminutive marble-topped *tocador* with a modest mirror for their daily shaving ritual. As expected, vain women had to boast a *tocador grande*, a marble-topped dresser with a full-length, gilt-framed mirror.

Spacious living rooms now had sofas and chairs that came en suite in the ponderous, albeit comfortable Fernando VII Style. The style became lighter as it adapted to Philippine tastes and is best exemplified by the *Cleopatra*, a daybed with scrolled arms. Its name harks back to Napoleon's conquest of Egypt and the Egyptian mania that swept Europe. Couches for reclining are even to this day known as Cleopatra although *divan* is interchangeably used.

Large circular tables, some an impressive twelve feet in diameter, became status symbols, for wood of such dimensions was not only rare and hard to come by, but had to be hauled at great expense from distant virgin forests. Long dining tables that could seat fourteen or more guests became common and were occasionally line-inlaid with *alintatao* and *kamagong*. Tables now proliferated in the *sala*, where *kamagong* centre tables with marble tops imported from Carrara were greatly admired, as were oval or oblong tables with pierced brass galleries around their tops. Wealth and leisure was accompanied with the appearance of chess tables. Smoking, a national pastime indulged in by all ages, required a *mesita pebetera*, literally 'a small table displaying a perfume burner', where a perpetually-burning joss stick not only scented the room but enabled one also to light-up one's Manila cigar. A tray, with the ingredients of a betel chew (*buyo*) or a cigar (*tabaco*), would be presented to valued visitors in a ritual of welcome.

Sideboards, which first appeared in Europe at the turn-of-the-century, made their entrance into Philippine dining rooms, which occasionally flaunted a cabinet of cutlery imported from Singapore. An *aparador para guardar vianda*, a larder, made its appearance in the kitchen, its feet resting on water-filled bowls to prevent ants from plundering its contents.

Chairs multiplied to the extent that in the 1850s some houses had as many as three-dozen armchairs. The comfortable rocking chair or *columpiyo* of mahogany or painted wood, introduced from Boston by American traders in the 1850s, quickly became popular as a status symbol, for its considerable size implied that one's home had ample space to accommodate chairs of that stature.

East of Suez

The opening of the Suez Canal in 1869 reduced the four-month journey from the Far East to Europe by half, opened a new market for Philippine abaca, sugar and indigo and made Britain the colony's largest trading partner. The ever-increasing number of European ships calling on local ports left their mark on Philippine architecture and design.

American clippers continued to bring ice from New England, as well as *sillas Americanas*, chairs of oak with caned seats and crested backs with incised carving. Popular in the 1870s, they are now called 'American Vienna' chairs, because they were assembled on arrival like their more popular bentwood Austrian counterparts. The *silla de Viena*, the first mass-produced knockdown furniture, was exported by the millions well into the 1920s, and could be seen in almost every home. Those with elaborately carved crests and armrests were the top of the line and could be found only in the most affluent of homes. Finished in brown, Filipinos preferred them in black.

Tables with marble tops were imported from China, but top-of-the-range came from Italy. Three to five feet in diameter, circular tables with ornately carved pedestals were items of envy, especially if the marble had grooved and fluted borders. It was considered imperative that the *lacena*, the dining room sideboard and the *trinchera*, the carving table with its back splashboard, had to have an Italian marble top – as did night tables in the bedroom and the *lavador con tocador* in the adjoining toilet.

In great demand was furniture created by the Chinese craftsman Ah Tay, the most fashionable carpenter of the day who laboured from the 1860s until the 1920s. His *narra* bedroom suites, particularly the intricately carved and canopied beds, were made to accommodate all sizes, from infant cribs to vast examples that could sleep four. The *aparador de tres lunas*, a huge, three-sectioned wardrobe with full-length mirrored doors, was the ultimate status symbol of any Philippine homestead followed by the towering *tocador grande*, which came to be called a *tremor* because its huge mirror literally trembled with every footstep.

Liberal and nationalist ideas imbibed by European-educated Filipinos bloomed into the 1896 Philippine Revolution against Spain, Asia's first revolution to counter a European power. It terminated Spanish dominion over the Philippines. However, before the Filipinos could achieve full independence, the American destruction of the Spanish Fleet at Manila Bay and the ensuing Spanish-American War forced Spain to relinquish its rights over its former colony and to sell the Islands to the United States, thereby triggering the Philippine-American War, which wreaked havoc on the economy and the countryside. The ensuing economic depression put an end to home construction and furniture making, and when the 20th century finally dawned, the sun rose on the first U.S. colony, which no longer focused on the culture of Europe but instead eyed the unrefined but modern world of the United States of America.

Right: A view of the *Caida* (music room) complete with harp, piano and chairs with backrest that resemble the shape of a violin – from the Museo De La Salle, Manila.

A library table of *narra* wood ably
supported by four fluted columns
terminating in C-scroll feet
connected by a pair of turned
and fluted stretchers.

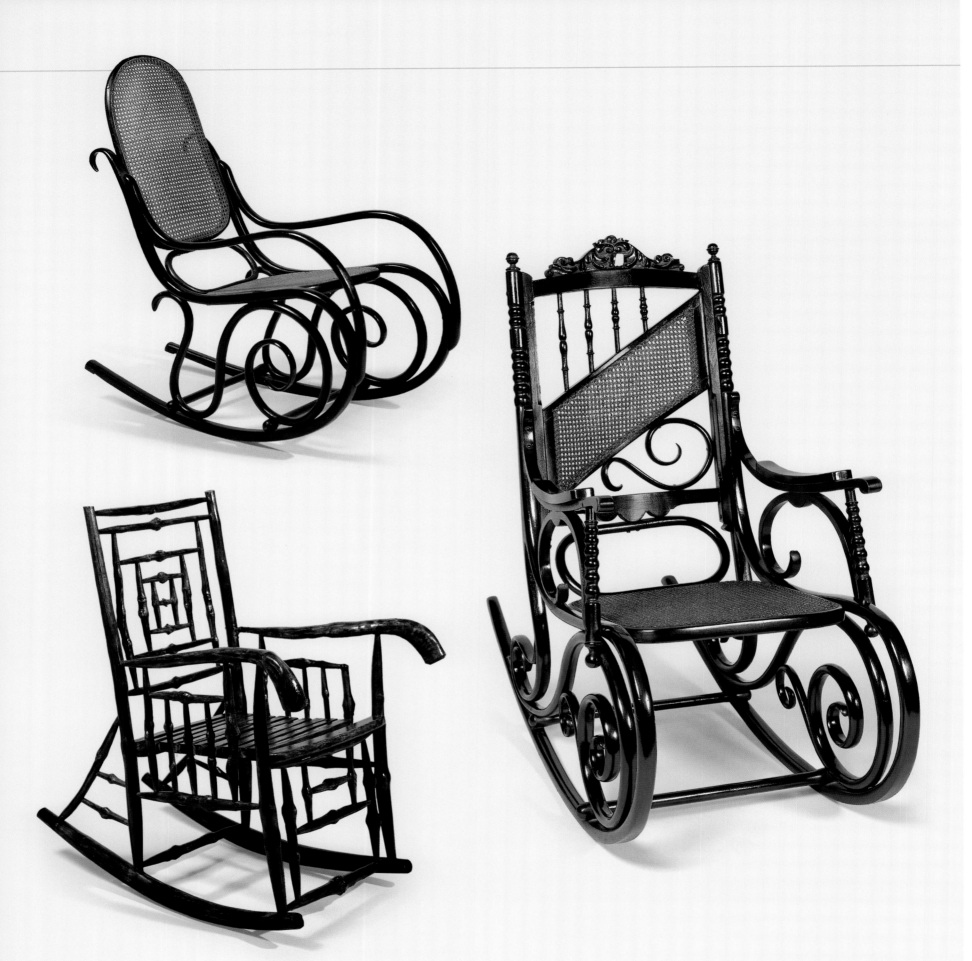

ASIAN
FURNITURE
PHILIPPINES

212

 Rocking chair, Vienna bentwood with backrest and seat of cane.

 An unusual rustic *columpiyo* (rocking chair) made from mangrove branches for outdoor use. Circa 1890.

 A bentwood rocking chair with caned seat and backrest. It is adorned with turned arm supports and back splats, sinuous lines and a carved crest. Austria. 1890s.

 Vienna bentwood *consola* (side table) with marble top. Austria. 1890s.

 Rocking chair of Viennese bentwood with caned seat and backrest, embellished with sinuous lines.

 Viennese bentwood settee with caned seat and elegantly rounded lines. Austria. 1890s.

Left: Ancestral portraits adorn the wall above a *narra* wood sofa with caned seat and double-caned arms and backrest in the *Fernando Septimo* or Spanish Empire style. 1830s.

 A *mariposa* (butterfly) sofa of *narra* wood with a caned seat and sinuous double-caned backrest and arms. The scrolled armrests are connected to the two front cabriole legs. The central scallop is embellished with intricate floral carving. 1860s.

 Sofa of *narra* wood with caned seat and a three-sectioned double-caned backrest with contoured supports. Foliate blossom-and-scrolls are carved on the arm supports, the seat apron and the front legs.

 Silla frailuna (friar's chair), now known as *sillon fraile*, of *narra* wood with wide armrests, caned seat and backrest, surmounted by an intricately carved and fretted crest. Circa 1850.

 Sillon fraile with caned backrest and seat. The crest on the flared back is decorated with carved foliate scrollwork. Turned baluster legs support the wide armrests.

 Sillon fraile of *narra* wood with caned seat and contoured backrest. The turned forelegs and gently curved rear legs are steadied by a plain H-stretcher.

 Silla perezosa (lounging chair) of *narra* wood with continuous caned seat and backrest surmounted with an interlocking pattern of flowering vines. The armrests are supported on brackets, while the legs are gently splayed. This particular style was a furniture staple in homes from the late 19th century until the 1930s.

PAMPANGA PROVINCE

Pampanga Province is located in the Central Luzon region and lies on the
northern shore of Manila Bay. It is the oldest of Central Luzon's seven provinces.
Farming and fishing are its primary industries, but the province also supports
thriving cottage industries in woodcarving, furniture and handicrafts. The
province has two distinct climates – it either rains or is dry.

LAGUNA PROVINCE

Laguna derives its name from La Laguna, 'the lake', the largest inland body of water in the Philippines, which also forms its northern boundary. The town of Calamba is the birthplace of the country's national hero, Jose Percival Rizal. Agriculture and fishing are its main industries but rice, sugarcane and fruit also contribute extensively to Laguna's economy. The province is the second largest producer of coconuts in the Philippines.

Carlos Trece narra wood side chair with tall vertical back framed by fluted columns with pointed finials, caned seat and double-caned backrest. The front legs are in hipped cabriole, while the rear legs are splayed.

Uniquely crafted Grandmother's chair with a fully caned, elongated backrest connecting to the seat which is supported by a sloping frame on both sides. The chair's crest is carved with floral design.

 High-backed *narra* wood armchair with a single caned seat and splayed armrests ending in scrolls. The double-caned backrest is framed by C-scroll carving. The turned legs are steadied by an X-stretcher topped with an urn finial.

 Armchair of *narra* wood with tall vertical back consisting of a double-caned oblong-shaped panel framed by a pair of twisted columns ending with pointed finials. The backrest is carved with foliate scrolls.

 Columpiyo (rocking chair) in the form of a neo-Louis XV *sillon* (planter's chair) in *narra* wood with caned seat continuing to an oval backrest. The splayed legs rest on plain rocking slats.

 Carlos Trece style rocking chair of *asana* wood with caned seat and double-caned back supported by turned side posts topped with finials. The extended armrests rest on and terminate in scrolls.

Victorian style *ante-sala* (lobby) circular table of *narra* wood with single, turned pumpkin-shaped baluster – centre support terminating with tripod claw feet.

Narra wood marble-topped round table with turned and carved cylindrical post with applied reed designs on the bottom and C-scroll pattern on the foliate-carved tripod legs.

BATANGAS PROVINCE

Batangas Province is located in southwestern Luzon. After devastating eruptions of the Taal Volcano in the 1700s, the ancient Taal town site was buried and the capital transferred to Batangas (now a city) in 1754, where it has remained to date. Linguists generally accept the province's name as meaning the 'Heart of the Tagalog Language'.

Square table of *tindalo* wood with a framed top. The claw-footed cabriole legs have grotesque masks carved on the knees. 1750s.

A delicately carved centre table of red and yellow varieties of *narra* wood with gracefully articulated aprons, turned legs and stretchers. Batangas Province. Late 18th century.

Table of *molave* wood with ball and claw-footed cabriole legs and benign grotesque masks on the knees. Pampanga Province. 18th century.

A large *comoda of narra* wood inlaid with bone and ebony and embellished with silver key escutcheons. The drawer knobs and pillars are also of ebony, and secret drawers are concealed behind the latter. Pampanga Province. Mid 19th century.

Opposite page: A lockable, three-drawer side table made of *tindalo* wood, inlaid with bone. Pampanga Province. 1830s.

Left: Five-drawer side table made of *tindalo* wood with drawer frame of *kamagong* wood ornamented by brass studs. The drawer faces are line-inlaid with *lanite* and carabao horn, while the side flanges and aprons are carved and fretted. Batangas Province. Circa 1800.

Three-drawer altar table of *tindalo* wood, inlaid with *lanite* and *kamagong*. Batangas Province. 1830s.

Five-drawer side or altar table made of *tindalo* wood and inlaid with *lanite* and bone. Batangas Province. Circa 1800.

Delicately carved, two-piece bookcase made of *kamagong* wood in the *Fernando Septimo* style. From Vigan City, Ilocos Sur Province. 1830s.

Identical pair of elaborately crested *aparadores de platera* (silverware cabinets) of *narra* wood. Each cabinet consists of four shelves – in this case heavily laden with plate. 1920s.

A *lavador con tocador* (combined dresser and washstand) with tilting mirror and marble shelves supported by a table of *narra* wood with turned and fluted legs and an X-stretcher tipped with an urn finial. Circa 1880.

Opposite page: *Aparador de tres lunas* (three-sectioned wardrobe) of *narra* wood with mirrored doors and three lower drawers.

 A *cuna* (child's crib) of *narra* wood with removable safeguards. This Ah Tay signature piece with its defined headboard could be found only in the wealthiest of households. The four finely carved bedposts and tester accommodate mosquito netting. Late 19th century.

Right: The interior of a lady's bedroom with walls painted with floral decoration in shades of old rose. The four-poster bed is graced with hand-embroidered old lace. Late 19th century.

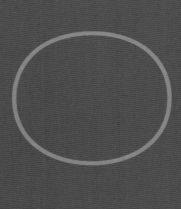

Its mountains seldom exceed 1,200 metres, but Korea is covered with them. Almost as tumultuous as its Precambrian geological formation were its successive political upheavals, for the peninsula long dangled like a plaything betwixt the dragon claws of encircling China to the north and west, and Japan to the east. Its alternating subjugation by both, instead of weakening the national character, forged and hardened a distinctively Korean identity, which owes much to linguistics scholar Ju Si-gyeong (1876–1914), who perfected the Hangul language with its unique characters, spelling and grammar.

Set high amid the famed "morning calm" mountains of South Korea stands Haeinsa Monastery, at the edge of Gyeongsang Province. Its upcurved blue-tiled roofs sweep majestically down the tiered hillside, like giant, broad-shouldered monks frozen in timeless meditation amid their mist-enveloped pine trees.

In times of stress, when Koreans need to escape from the cities and calm their volatile temperaments, it is retreats like this to which they retire to quiet their troubled psyche. The monasteries Koreans hold so dear are their social escape valves, essential for that balance that restores the harmony of their lives.

Haeinsa Monastery, whose name derives from the Korean phrase for "reflection on a smooth sea", is especially revered, for it holds a complete set of the *Tripitaka Koreana*, the collected writings of Mahayana Buddhism. Though most Buddhist countries in East Asia possess a copy of the *Tripitaka*, the Korean edition at Haeinsa is considered the best.

Korean artisans wrapped the furniture around the wood, and not the wood around the furniture.

Carved in the 13th century, this consists of 52,382,960 characters inscribed on 81,258 double-sided woodblocks in 6,802 volumes. It was commissioned by the government-in-exile, to replace an identical set destroyed in 1232 by Mongol invaders. The original set had taken 77 years to complete, and was not finished until 1087. King Kojong ordered the set remade, and work on this replacement commenced in 1236. It was felt that this arduous task of renewing the entire *Tripitaka* would convince Buddha to intervene and help repel the Mongolian invaders.

The woodblocks were made of white birch, first soaked in sea water for three years, then boiled and dried for three more years. Only then could work commence on the painstaking task of planning and carving them with their 52 million *Hanja* characters. The work was undertaken on Kanghwa Island, and the complete library was moved to Haeinsa during the early years of the Yi Dynasty.

Demanding such extremes of patient attention, this act of faith exemplifies the Korean love for the exquisite art of wood working. It also explains the perfection of Korean furniture.

The traditional Korean cabinet maker possessed an almost spiritual affinity with the wood under his plane. He loved it for its grain, in which he read its history. Trees several hundred years old spoke to him of their own meditations and of the songs they had gleaned from their close relationships with sunlight, earth, wind and rain.

A tree that had matured that long had derived the very essence of its being through its roots in the native soil, developing its distinctive form and patina through absorbing water and nutrients in the course of its long lifetime, and by engaging in deep, unspoken conversations with the elements. Such a tree might be destined to fall and die, but its soul could endure forever through the texture of its grain.

It was this instinct that guided the carpenter's tools, executing his belief that the wood was more than a mere source of the material needed to complete the work at hand. It *was* the work at hand, and the particular piece of furniture which it composed served merely as the vehicle for its form.

The severity of Korean winters dictated rooms that were small and low-ceilinged, generally heated by hot water running under tiled floors. Hence Korean furniture evolved to fit within these confines, modest, sparing and ground-hugging in its general configuration but almost jewel-like in its detail. To dwell in such a room, in touch with such furniture, is to understand what is meant by that defining attribute of morning calm. If one listens very, very carefully, one can almost hear the sound of one hand clapping.

Previous page: Cast from coins donated by the nation, and modelled on the Bell of King Songdok, dating from 771AD, the massive Korean Bell of Friendship is set in a pagoda-like structure. Opposite page: (Upper) The graceful granite staircase of Pulguk-sa temple, one of the most revered spiritual retreats in Korea, built in 535 AD. (Lower left) A rural village homestead. (Lower right) Door gods in traditional Korean costume are carved from granite.

A Hidden Treasury of Korean Furniture

Anthony Banks

Korea is lodged, sometimes ill fatedly, between two vastly different neighbours, Japan and China. It is therefore not especially surprising that Korea's furniture tradition, like other aspects of her culture, is often viewed as nestling somewhere between those of its two neighbours in terms of origin and style. However, though the very earliest examples of Choson period (1392–1910) wood crafts illustrated in paintings show Ming Chinese influences up until the 17th century, Young-kyu Park, Professor of Fine Art at Young-in University notes that a distinctive Korean style had already emerged by the 18th century.

Whilst one can say that Korean furniture is uniquely 'Korean', how is this uniqueness to be defined? How can one use it to comprehend the differences between the Korean tradition and those of her two influential neighbours? The chief difference seems to lie not just in the materials employed – the wood itself, but also in what the wood represented and how it was employed. Korean artisans eschewed artifice in favour of nature. They wrapped the furniture around the wood, not the wood around the furniture. The natural beauty of the wood was the principal canvas upon which the craftsman focused his attention. Wherever possible, the artisan attempted to reproduce the wider physical landscape in miniature on the flat surfaces of the wood used. Often it is possible to envisage mountain ranges and hills in the grain of the wood. Similarly, we see evidence of artisans going to great lengths, and no doubt expense for their patrons, to ensure that wood surfaces retain and even emphasise their original pattern and grain.

In addition, the woods themselves, if properly appreciated, provide a window into Choson society. Earthy, Oriental red pine was favoured by the wealthy and penurious alike for its reflection of the Confucian exhortation to pursue a life both simple in taste and noble in nature. Elm wood, and its cousin, Northern Elm root, or 'dragon wood' ('*Yong-Mok*' in Korean) – named for the impression it creates of dragons swirling in endless skies – were favoured by the affluent, and reflected the nobility, wealth and perhaps even the aspirations of its owners. Paulownia, lightweight and insect resistant and therefore utilitarian, can be used, when split correctly, to produce beautiful mirror images. The seemingly humble bamboo was favoured not only as a subject of literati paintings but also as the medium for producing brush pots, writing implements and other accoutrements of the gentleman scholar. Its value derived from its height and straightness, perceived as reflecting Confucian moral precepts that advocated a simple, upright life.

The Influence of Korean Architecture on Furniture Design

There is an intimate relationship between furniture and architecture, and like all furniture, there is a kinship between Choson furniture and the physical spaces within which it was designed. Chinese and Western interiors tend to be large and spacious, with high ceilings – an arrangement of space entirely appropriate to cultures that are not floor based. With the exception of a few particularly grand houses, Choson architecture was characterised by smaller rooms, and furniture thus had to be less visually obtrusive and smaller in order not to take up too much of the limited living space. More importantly, Korea's home culture depended to a great extent on the comfort derived from the use of under floor central heating (*ondol*), which gave rise to a furniture that was convenient for use at floor height.

A Brief Social History of Korean Furniture

But *which* Korean traditional furniture are we talking about? From the mid 19th century to the period of Japanese colonial rule, Korean furniture went through a rapid and dramatic series of changes that must be taken into account if we are to distinguish between variations in quality, function, provenance and authenticity. Choson furniture features simple, smooth and flowing lines, with plain but elegant decorations that highlight the inherent beauty of its basic structure. The furniture from the colonial period, on the other hand, reflects both the influence of changes to the consumer base, as well as the switch to limited mass production in small factories and workshops to accommodate a wider but less discriminating buying public. Designs, formerly respected for their strict observance to long established and highly sophisticated pattern work, and bounded by an overwhelming need for simplicity and sobriety, became increasingly opulent and stylised.

A *Mori-jang* cabinet provides an Asian grace note in a contemporary western home.

Therefore, rather than attempting to corral all of the traditional furniture of Korea into the general catchall designation of 'late Choson', it is necessary to take a few moments to subdivide it into more specific sub categories.

Classical or Representative Choson. Over 150 years old. Between the development of a truly unique Korean style of furniture by the 18th century, and the last two decades of the 19th century, Korean furniture remained consistent in design and metal pattern work, with regions and cities adhering to their own traditions and styles. Because such pieces maintain a virtually uninterrupted continuity of style and form, one can safely say that they represent the highest form of the tradition and are thus much sought after by Korean curators, collectors and dealers. Most furniture within this category is approximately 150 years old or even older. Dae-young Chung, a noted scholar, author and collector estimates that less than 5% of the classic furniture currently in museums, university collections and prestigious homes falls within this category.

Transitional Choson. Approximately 120–150 years old. Dramatic and far-reaching societal changes occurred in Korea during the last two decades of the 19th century – changes that were reflected in furniture and the other decorative arts, particularly painting and ceramics. Yangban, the scholar aristocrat class, was beginning to decline in wealth and influence, and the itinerant artisans who had traditionally catered to the Yangban found themselves with fewer and fewer patrons. These dedicated artisans had passed down their knowledge of construction techniques and regional metal pattern work to their apprentices for generations, but as Korean society changed and the aristocracy fell into decline, formerly unbroken lineages of style and tradition began to be eroded. The artisans drifted into the cities where their knowledge and traditions began to be diluted.

Folk period or vulgarized pieces. Turn of the century. The increasing wealth of the general population, coupled with the decline in Yangban fortunes, created new markets for furniture, which had previously been affordable only to the elite classes. However, many of these *nouveau riche* collectors were either unfamiliar or unconcerned with the symbolism of the furniture's metal work. This accelerated the dilution of skills and lack of adherence to 'classical' designs among the rapidly disappearing artisans and their apprentices. Though such pieces date from the late Choson, they frequently contain hybrid metal pattern work from more than one region or style. They are, to some extent, interpretations of 'classical' Choson pieces.

Post-Colonial period. The furniture of this period, can be further subdivided as follows:
- Innocuous copies; unpretentious pieces which are an unselfconscious extension of folk or colonial period styles, or indeed furniture built in the traditional manner, perhaps with an older original example as a model or at least as a guiding influence.
- Remade furniture. These pieces show evidence of having been reconstructed from a number of other pieces in extreme disrepair. Their abundance in the market creates difficulties in evaluating authenticity for the uninitiated observer.

- Restored furniture. Exact placement within any timeline remains a fluid and somewhat subjective matter for 'restored' furniture; pieces which remain 'genuine' to varying degrees, but have nevertheless undergone extensive repairs and 'restoration', the extent of which can be so great as to erode the integrity of the piece. Dae-young Chung, the noted authority on this subject, argues that any alterations which involve the replacement or repairs to any part of a piece of original furniture which is essential to its *'seng myong'*, or 'essence' have a profound effect upon its collectability and market value.

The Characteristics of Choson Dynasty Furniture

While Chinese furniture possesses its own Bible of connoisseurship, the Korean tradition possesses no such definitive roadmap of classic style.

What we do have to guide us, however, is the remaining furniture itself. If we are able to categorise the furniture according to function, age and provenance, then we can begin to understand the parameters of style we should be looking for. In other words, we come closer to being able to mirror the aesthetic criteria originally used to evaluate this furniture.

The best examples of Choson furniture are rectangular in form, with surfaces that are often simply decorated. Sobriety and restraint were favoured characteristics in Confucianism and a family of taste and breeding would have attempted to convey these qualities in the way their home was furnished as well. This is not to say that high quality pieces are not, at times, artfully decorated with gorgeous lacquer, mother-of-pearl and elaborate metal work; however, the highest forms of the tradition certainly demonstrate an aesthetic of minimalism and simplicity.

Interiors of the home of renowned Korean architect Suh Se-Ok and his wife Min-ja Chung, faithfully preserve the heritage of Korea's cultural past.

What should be emphasised is that a great deal of attention was paid to *propriety* – the structural proportion of furniture. It is often not possible, for example, to determine the actual physical size of well-proportioned pieces by simply studying a photograph or drawing, since the full impact of the masterful balance of metal work and grain of the wood defies exact measurement. Understanding the skills of joinery and carpentry no doubt enhances the connoisseurship of Korean furniture, and it is true that the techniques employed play an important part in the overall effect of elegantly harmonious proportions. However, we are painting a vast landscape with a very broad brush, and scholars such as Edward Reynolds Wright and Man Sill Pai have undertaken detailed research into this intriguing aspect of Korean furniture. Suffice it to say that one of the many charming construction techniques is the use of floating panels. Used in many cabinets, such panels allow the furniture to accommodate the wood's natural expansion and contraction due to changes in humidity, and thereby serve to prevent fissures and warping.

Types of Furniture

A truly vast range of furniture types is still available. Large furnishings can be divided into the following categories: coffers and chests (*kwei* or *bandaji*), stackable cabinets in varying sizes (*nong*), and cabinets with two or more built-in compartments within a single frame (*jang*). *Jang* can be further subdivided into headside chests (*mori-jang*), as well as cabinets for the storage of important ceremonial or official garments, gowns, headwear and uniforms. Add to these smaller, portable chests (sometimes erroneously grouped together as wedding chests (*h'am*)), as well as small tables and stationary boxes used by the aristocracy, and we have a formidably varied landscape of woodcraft and design. The word *kwei* (meaning chest) is used to refer to coffers both large and small with a top opening door as well as those chests now known as *bandaji* (chests with an opening extending half way across the front of the piece).

One way to categorise these types more narrowly is according to function; which again requires reference to not only the architectural but also the social and class parameters of late Choson Korea. Many coffers or *bandaji* were indeed used by all classes to store ubiquitous items such as clothing, household incidentals and coins (Choson currency consisted of large and unwieldy strings of coins, and affluent households would have required one or more of these heavy coffers. Their size and weight, as well as the quality of the materials used, would have reflected the relative wealth and social standing of their owners). Many dealers refer to *bandaji* as blanket chests; however, seasonal bedding was simply folded and stacked on the floor or on the nearest and most conveniently sized chest. *Nong* and *jang* were primarily used to store clothing, wedding mementos, stationary or women's incidentals and makeup.

Within each general category of furniture, there were items designed for specific needs, including those related to scrolls, manuscripts and books. Since only an estimated 5% of the Choson population was both literate and wealthy enough to need and own such items, this furniture is correspondingly rare, even more so since these are among the pieces most prized by knowledgeable Korean curators and connoisseurs.

This leads to another factor determining function that is intimately related to the culture of Choson Korea and how that culture was reflected in its architecture: the issue of gender. The sexes were strictly separated in Choson Korea, a separation that was rigidly enforced not only in social practices but also within the physical spaces families inhabited.

In upper class households, females and males lived apart, and their furniture naturally had different forms and functions. In the female quarters, furniture consisted largely of clothing chests and boxes. Lighter, more feminine motifs, often those associated with fertility, such as bats, embellished such pieces. Grain, bean and rice chests, both large and small, were generally located in the kitchen area, as were large, rustically finished pantry shelves used for the storage of preserves and other cooking implements.

Korean architect Suh Se-Ok modelled his contemporary home on a 200-year-old Yi Dynasty residence at Seoul's Changdong Palace.

In contrast, the furniture found in the Confucian gentleman-scholar's rooms reflected his *métier* – the pursuit of learning and the entertainment of friends or valued guests. Elegant headside chests, scroll cases and book chests, writing and sutra tables were placed artfully in his study, each subdued, sober and restrained in character and containing necessities such as stationary items and books, and providing a platform for the display of fine ceramics, calligraphy brushes or scholar's rocks.

Regional Styles

Consistency amidst diversity – this best describes one of the most distinctive and important features of late Choson and early 20th century Korean chests: regional style. Variations in regional style consist of differences, both dramatic and subtle, in metal pattern work from city to city, and region to region.

The diversity of metal work patterns, proportion and design within a comparatively small geographic area is remarkable. Styles can generally be identified by their distinctive metal pattern work, which varies according to the region. Some of the most commonly encountered regional styles are those of

Kyongi, Cholla, Kyongsang, Chungchong and Kanghwa, in the south, and Bakchon, Pyongyang and Kaesong in the north. However, within these very broad categories each district or even each city also had its own style of metal work and patterns. Whilst it is possible to contend that styles within a province had very general similarities, the variations within each province according to city or district mean that reliance upon provincial origin is simply too crude a tool when categorizing Korean chests.

Consider, for example the varieties displayed within the province of Cholla. Like other provinces, it can be broadly sub-divided according to the cities around which strong regional variations in metal work patterns and styles developed. The Chonju chests of Cholla Province are extremely rare and can command prices in the tens of thousands of dollars, whereas, for the time being at least, chests in the main style known as Cholla remain relatively common and therefore command less of a premium in terms of collectability and value.

Turning to chests from North Korea, we see variations that are quite stark. Among the most popular chests with collectors are those in the monumental Bakchon style, which are far larger than those from other areas. Even more distinctive, however, is their elaborate metal work, known as *sung-sung-ni*. This refers to the use of large sheets of metal decoration that have been very heavily perforated to create intricate patterns and designs – the most common feature being a large, centrally placed motif of the South Gate of the capital. The other commonly encountered North Korean chest is the Pyongyang style chest, which is quite unique. These chests are characterized by white brass bands that often cover almost the entire face of the chest – interesting given the general preoccupation by craftsmen and consumers alike with the natural beauty and grain of the woods used. These chests, however, do not seem to be as popular with connoisseurs and collectors, who tend to seek out and acquire pieces from the South instead.

Lacquerware

Many craftsmen took great pride in the quality of lacquer finishing used on their products – the most common form being red or brown natural lacquer (*ot-chil*), using sap extracted from a lacquer tree (*ot-namu*). An original patina implies that it will be easier to judge the age of a piece of furniture. Korean collectors prefer an original patina, if at all possible, even if this means purchasing a piece in its original 'used' condition, or one which otherwise looks as if it has seen better days.

Metal Work

Chests or coffers made in the classical tradition (or at least those that are not contemporary) will have hand-beaten metal work and fittings. As such, they should exhibit the roughness and irregular lines associated with this method of production. In the case of North Korean *sung-sung-ni* metal work, however, most colonial or early 20th century pieces have stamped metal work. Older North Korean pieces, as well as Kyongi Province pieces featuring *sung-sung-ni* metal work, can fortunately still be found with hand-beaten fittings, and command prices accordingly.

Considerations for Collectors

Forgery is a continuing issue in most fields of collecting, and furniture is by no means an exception to this phenomena. It is an irritant to the uninitiated and to the seasoned collector alike, deterring novices from entering the market and infuriating collectors who realise only too late that a treasured piece of is in fact only a few decades old.

Unrealistic Expectations

Korea's modern history has been tumultuous, to say the least. Our period of interest, which stretches from the late Choson to the present, has seen monumental change. In terms of war alone, the first Sino-Japanese war of 1894–1895, the Russo Japanese war of 1904–1905, and the horrendously destructive 1950–1953 Korean War, have been fought on Korean soil. Various rebellions, peasant uprisings, and the large-scale acquisition of cultural assets by colonial administrators can be added to the list of events that reduced the quantity of high quality furniture still in existence. Post-war economics and social change have also played their part in ways to a great extent mirrored in the Japanese post-war experience.

From the late post-war period until the onset of the bubble economy in Japan, a great many articles of Japanese cabinetry (*dansu*), valuable Edo period pieces and less valuable Taisho or Showa period pieces, were sold off or simply discarded. These were the boom times for Westerners who found themselves entranced by this furniture. The bubble economy coincided with a reemerging interest amongst many Japanese, causing a rise in prices, which had a dramatic effect on the market.

Much the same process occurred in Korea as Richard Christenson noted:

"This period in the early 70's was a dangerous time for Korean antiques. They were an endangered species, too old to be seen as useful in everyday life, but not yet old or rare enough to be treasured as antiques, and so, many Koreans sold them quite readily to the merchants from Seoul who also combed the countryside. Some families just threw the old things away.

A 19th century Korean cabinet shelves classic literary works, together with calligraphy brushes and other scholarly items.

A Korean friend related a day in the 1960s in his rural home when old wooden chests were happily discarded and replaced by shiny new furniture made of imitation wood or plastic. That night the old chests were broken up and burned in the courtyard – a bonfire celebrating the symbolic release from dark penury, a delivery toward the early dawn of modernity and its promise of comfort. These days many Koreans treasure such antiques, and those that remain are carefully preserved, but still the question lingers, 'How much was lost?'"

It is quite acceptable in the West to encounter pieces of furniture that are several hundred years old. This is sadly not the case in Korea. Although much furniture remains on the market in Korea, a great many of the genuine pieces in private hands were manufactured during the colonial period, when semi-mass production had begun to take a firm hold. In fact, it has been estimated that pieces made in the classical tradition (between 120–150 years old or older) constitutes less than 5% of those on the market.

There are hierarchies in all things and antique furniture dealers are no exception. The knowledge and expertise of any given dealer correlates to a great extent with more cautious and conservative estimates of age. Reputable dealers will also be more willing to make finer distinctions in age rather than using the over-used generalisation of 'Choson Dynasty' – there is Choson and then there is *Choson*. Korean cabinetry and chests have their own laws and sacred geometry of aesthetic evaluation. They can be measured from the coarse to the exquisite and all gradients and shades of quality in between. Exemplary dealers will be able to advise whether an item of furniture is late Choson, earlier Choson, colonial period or post-war.

Korea's recent history is reflected in her furniture as much as it is in the dwindling number of Koreans who were part of the monumental changes which have accompanied Korea in her modern journey. These changes are reflected as much in what remains of Korea's furniture tradition as in what has sadly been lost.

CHOLLA

Cholla Province is located in southwestern South Korea. Its coastline, which includes nearly 2,000 islands, most uninhabited, is roughly 3,800 miles (6,100 km) long. The province's eastern part is dominated by mountain ranges covered with dense forests, offering the ROK its prime source of timber. Agricultural plains occupy western Cholla, dubbed the 'food basket' of Korea, the country's primary rice-growing province.

Whagak *mori-jang.* Two-door headside chest used for the storage of nightclothes and accessories, commonly found in the private quarters of Korean homes. The front façade is adorned with thin plates of red stained ox horn. Metal ornaments in the shape of butterflies supplement the overall decoration.

Two-door, *mori-jang* or headside chest of cherry wood floating panels with a dark lime wood frame and yellow brass fittings in the North Korean style of Kaesong. Late 19th century.

Bandaji, commonly referred to as blanket chest typical of Pyongyang City. Constructed of lime wood, conspicuously embellished with white brass fittings. The incised designs on the brass include auspicious phoenix and bat motifs. North Korea. 19th century.

Bandaji or blanket chest: Rectangular repository with an upper half-door that opens forward. Blackened metal embellishments dominate the front façade. Lime wood. Kyongi Province. Early 19th century.

Bandaji, or blanket chest. Used also to store manuscripts, documents or utensils required for ceremonies related to ancestor worship. Cholla Province. Late 19th century.

 Mori-jang – headside chest commonly located in the private quarters of Korean homes. Four-drawer, two-door red and black lacquer cabinet with yellow brass adornments. The footrest with stretchers and carved lower apron safeguards the chest from floors heated in winter. Kyongi Province. Late 19th century.

Right: Detail of chest-on-chest. Zelkova (elm wood) frame with circular brass hinges and fittings, cherry wood panels inlaid with persimmon wood in mirror patterns. Kyongi Province. Late 19th century.

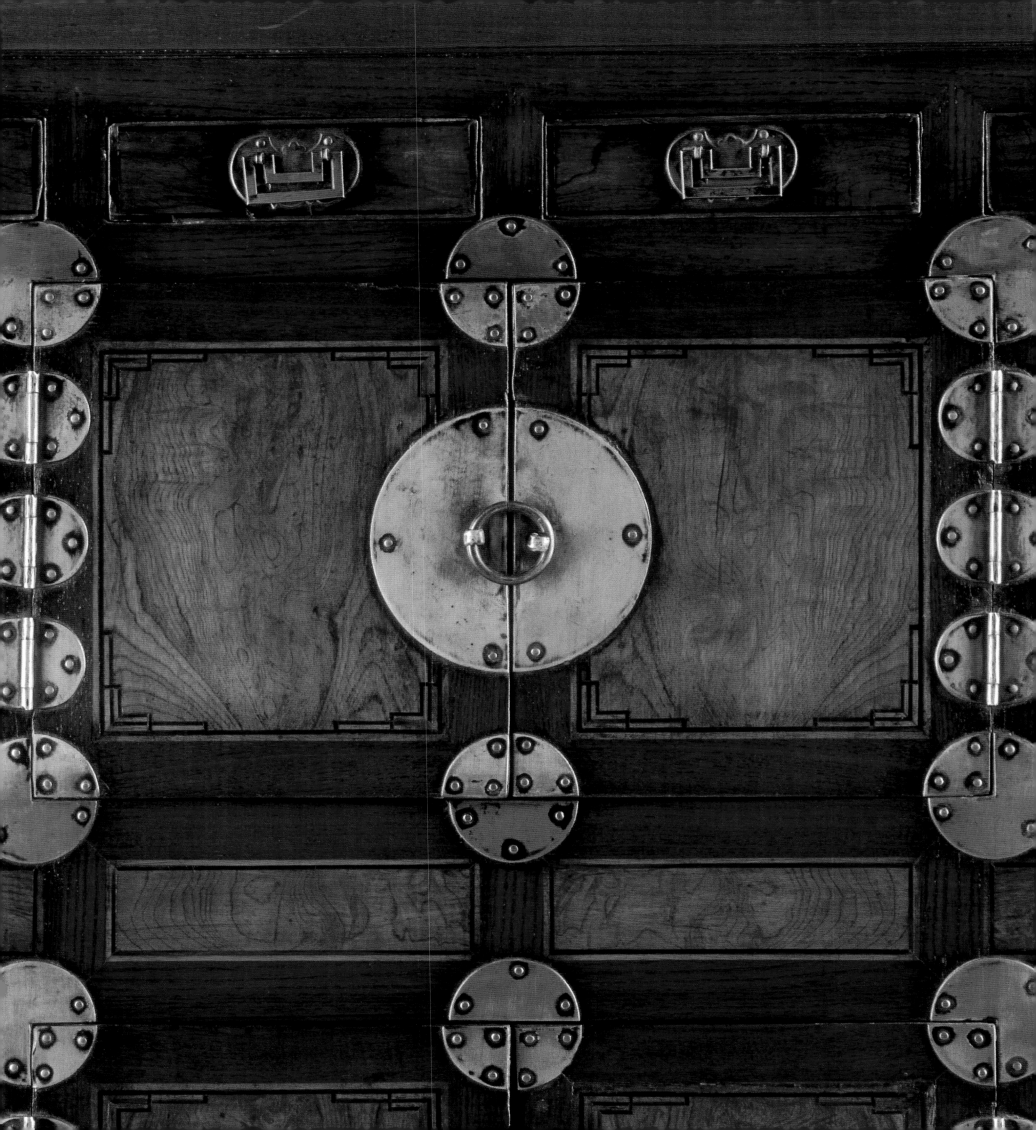

Kanghwa *bandaji* or blanket repository. Rectangular chest made of zelkova boards of natural wood tones. Cast iron ornamentation enhances the front façade. During the long Korean winters chests are raised on footrests to protect against cracking from heated floors. Kanghwa Island. 19th century.

Mori-jang, headside chest with four drawers and two doors made of cherry wood with brass fittings. The cabinet stands on a footrest with a plain apron. The ornaments of brass and nickel alloy display symbols of prosperity and happiness. Kyongsang Province. Late 19th century.

Mori-jang, headside chest of four drawers and two doors made of cherry wood with white brass fittings and double-lock centre plate. Bat motifs resembling butterflies decorate the drawer pullers. Kyongsang Province. Late 19th century.

Mungap *mori-jang*; stationery-combination headside chest commonly located in private quarters of Korean homes. Thin frame, T-shaped braces of brass and finely rendered bat motif hinges combine to create a cabinet of pleasing proportions. Kyongi Province. 19th century.

Bandaji blanket chest. Masculine in character, this rectangular chest is made of sturdy pine wood of natural honey colour tones. The chest is characterised by fine, *sung-sung-ni* (lace-like) ironwork from the remote Bakchon area. North Korea. Mid 19th century.

 Two-tiered cabinet of elm wood with twelve drawers. Each drawer, narrow in width, is tall and deep. Specifically adapted for the Western export market. Seoul. Contemporary.

 *Ich'ung-jang.* Two-tiered clothing cabinet with interlocking panels of polished cherry wood. Decorated with white metal hinges and lock plate fittings. During Korea's long winters chests are placed on foot stands to insulate against cracking from heated floors. Cholla Province. Mid 19th century.

 Yichung-jang. Bi-level kitchen cabinet with slatted ribs to allow for ventilation – in modern times commonly adapted as bookcase. The hinged side panels allow for swing-doors to be further extended, providing access to the cabinet's entire width to store scrolls, Kyung Ki Province. Early 19th century.

Bandaji, blanket chest. Masculine in appearance and constructed of sturdy pine in honey colour tones. The upper portion of the front façade is hinged and opens forward. *Sung-sung-ni* (lace-like) ironwork characterises the cabinet from Bakchon area. North Korea. Mid 19th century.

 Two-tiered *Pandaji-weigori-jang* uniform cabinet with front façade decorated with white metal fittings. Two upper doors have ventilation slats. Lower section has half panel door which opens forward, secured by large lock plate. Rosewood. North Kyongsang Province. Late 18th century.

 Sanch'ung-jang. Three-tiered lady's clothing cabinet decorated with brass fittings in butterfly motif, symbolising conjugal felicity. The butterfly is a common decorative symbol applied also in embroidery and chinaware. Elm wood with yellow brass fittings. Chen Ra Nam Province. Late 19th century.

 Tall cupboard made of dark pine wood with minimal brass work. Hinged doors enclose the upper compartment, while sliding doors seclude the lower section. Side stretchers connect front and back legs. Made for Western export market. Seoul. Contemporary.

 Kwanbok-jang, wardrobe. The upper compartment consists of textile-backed latticework doors to allow for ventilation. The cabinet is composed of two compartments within a single frame. Rosewood. Kyongi Province. 20th century.

Right: Contemporary home interior displays three-tiered lady's storage chest. Fashioned from multi panels of cherry wood, the grain of which is arranged and set symmetrically. Butterfly motifs decorate the brass lock plates. Kyongi Province. Early 20th century.

Left: *Samchung-jang:* Tall, three-tiered household cabinet of zelkova wood. The frame is of polished pine wood and decorated with dulled metal fittings. This form of classic cabinet was widely reproduced in the early 1970s, when Korean furniture first became fashionable in the West. Kyongi Province. Contemporary.

Scholar's book cabinet with three compartments and protruding headboard. The persimmon wood façade is artfully assembled to emphasise the mirror image of its dark grain. Doors have minimal metal embellishments. Chen Ra Nam Province. Contemporary.

Dining room cabinet used for the storage of silverware and cutlery. Elm wood *(nurup namu)* with yellow brass fittings. Seoul. Contemporary.

Ich'ung-nong. Two-unit stacked chest. This finely constructed cabinet with mother-of-pearl door inlays and gentle embellishments of brass is by design a lady's cabinet. The footrest is removable when floor heating in winter is no longer in use. Chungchong Province. Late 19th century.

Chaek-bandaji. Book cabinet. A superlative example of Korean cabinet making. Pine wood applied to the cabinet's framework is offset by panels of zelkova root. The wood is accented by the intricate yet subdued yellow brass metal work. Kyongsang Province. 19th century.

GYEONGGI

Gyeonggi Province is located in Korea's central western plains, and surrounds the capital city, Seoul. The province is a vast fertile valley along the Han River that has been settled since prehistoric times. Its close proximity to Seoul has made it a centre of both heavy industry and a base for the manufacture and restoration of furniture.

Yichung-jang. Bi-level chest displays masterly Korean craftsmanship in the use of subtle wood grain on the cabinet's front façade. The chest is of zelkova root, renowned for its distinctive grain and is ornamented with polished brass fittings. Cholla Province. 19th century.

Prized example of a three-tiered cabinet, in distinctive red and black lacquer finish. In times gone by this technique was exclusive to the former extended royal family. Zelkova root. Kyongi Province. 19th century.

Samchung-jang. Three-level chest made of persimmon wood with pronounced metal ornamentation. Twin doors concealed the storage of clothing, while accessories were retained in the drawers. Elm wood. Kanghwa Island. Early 20th century.

Right: With its red pine beams and highly polished floor, the sparsely furnished living room of the famed Korean architect Suh Se-Ok, and his wife Min-ja Chung, accurately preserves the heritage of Korea's architectural past.

Soban. Rectangular tray-tables used to serve light snacks and tea, rather than full meals. The legs are in cabriole style, known in Korea as 'tiger' legs *(hochokban)* and are connected by side stretchers. These tray-tables are in everyday use throughout the Korean Peninsula.

 Chukjol-ban. Rectangular tray-table with hump-back stretcher and imitation bamboo-formed legs. Zelkova wood with lacquered table surface. South Cholla Province. 19th century.

 Chukjol-ban. Rectangular table with lacquered zelkova wood tray top. A wide carved apron runs along all four sides. An upper and two lower side stretchers connect the *'ginkgo'* rope-twine design legs. South Cholla Province. Early 20th century.

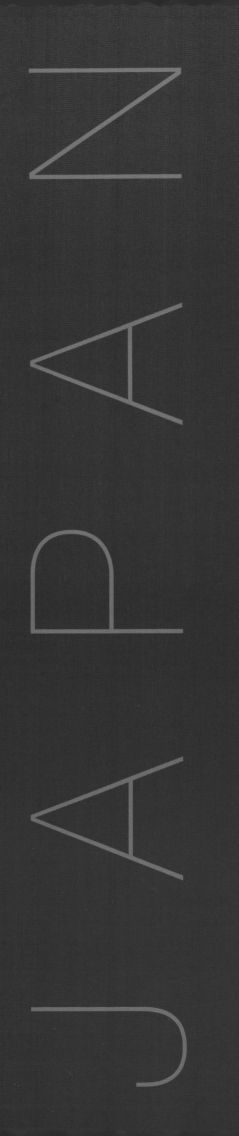

JAPAN

Although much of its cultural roots and even its writing stemmed from China, Japan remains the very epitome of insularity, keeping its metaphorical distance from neighbouring Asian countries it formerly invaded and subjugated. In 1603, a Tokugawa shogunate ushered in a long period of isolation from foreign influence. For 250 years this policy enabled Japan to enjoy stability and a flowering of its indigenous culture. Here refinement of thought, gesture, costume, art and architecture were brought to an apotheosis of elegance that found its culmination in the tea ceremony and in the spiritual mysteries of Shintoism and Zen Buddhism.

Ordinary Japanese possessed no furniture that would have been recognised as such in the western world. They sat on cushions, ate at low tables and slept on futons laid over tatami matting.

An inverted map of Eurasia will reveal Japan's near mirror image bordering the Atlantic rather than the Pacific, and separated from the continental land mass by the English Channel rather than the Sea of Japan. Both archipelagos have much in common, their insularity breeding a species of disdain for their continental neighbours.

Inevitably, however, history breached their separateness, in Britain's case infiltrating its defences with the offshoots of the Roman and Norman conquests and in Japan's case injecting the influence of a much older civilisation stemming from China. To this day neither recipient willingly admits its debt to that cultural provenance.

Japan planted its inherited roots in its native soil, pruned them, pollinated them, grafted indigenous seedlings on to them and nurtured them like ancient and venerable bonsai until they matured into distinctively Japanese hybrids as far removed as possible from their progenitors. But the fact remains that, if we know enough to read one language, we can read, and at least partly understand, the other.

As with scroll painting, pottery, carvings, Buddhist temples and venerated deities, the same is true of Japanese furniture. While admiring the uniquely Japanese aesthetic, we can discern the underlying ancestry. It is what their inimitable temperament has made of it that transfigures and elevates the end result for, living close to nature, with Shinto beliefs intermingled with their Zen Buddhist faith, the Japanese have perfected the art of opposites, of blending complexity with simplicity, of finding more in less.

When we enter a traditional – as distinct from a modern – Japanese home, however small it may be spatially, we enter a microcosm self-contained and absolute. As with that parallel society on the far side of the planet, the Japanese householder subscribes to the Englishman's tenet that his home is his castle.

Wherever the site is large enough, the house itself is enclosed in a fenced garden – even though the width of this may be barely enough to permit passage between the wall and the fence. And however two-dimensional in reality, the garden will seem, viewed from the windows, a three-dimensional vista of bamboo and – though minimal in extent – artfully arranged 'landscape' of moss, rocks, fern and running water.

The transition from garden to interior is less a separation than a symbiosis. Shedding footwear at the stoop, we pass into another dimension of the same ethos, still surrounded by artifacts that reinforce the prevailing reverence for nature, that all pervading affinity with the bedrock, the very soul of Japan.

The *tatami* floors are of rush mat, beautifully woven and springy as turf underfoot, the interior walls are of gossamer thin rice paper, imprinted with patterns of leaf and bough, moon and willow. But most of all it is the furniture that reminds us we are not only at home but at peace with the primal source from which we sprang.

The grain of the wood, wherever possible, allows the original shape to dictate the finished contours. This is furniture less concerned with the overall effect than with the detail, less preoccupied with grandeur than with grace. Ultimately, it is furniture that invites, and repays, closer scrutiny, for like the country that produced it – that distinct world within a world – this too holds the promise that, if one can only read between the grain, one may finally interpret the rubric and plumb its secrets.

Worlds within the Japanese Home

Edited by Yokobori Yoichi

Dusk gathers around the skirts of suburban Edo. The tired rays of the setting autumnal sun try weakly to spar with kindling fires indoors. The teashop owner and his wife are busy piling fresh slivers of wood into the *irori* hearth built into the floor and nudging it on with scoops of fat. Guests pass under a new pair of *noren* entrance curtains that cover the upper half of the heavy sliding doors along the wide rectangular frontage. They pass by low tables set around the *irori* and into a private chamber. The air is thick with the damp odours of lard and wood, against a background of fresh-mown *igusa* rush wafting from the *tatami* mats covering the wooden floor. The warm glow of a lone lamp on the far side, placed before a Buddhist deity, lights up the passage.

One cannot see beyond the *shoji* panels of trellised wood papered over on the inside. Light from different sources – the sneaking rays of the sun, the crackling tongues of flame in the *irori*, the glowering coals of the *hibachi*, and the throw of the lamp on the passage – suffuses through the *shoji* and casts a blend of cosy orange and yellow over the *byobu*. Painted exquisitely with animal and bird motifs, the authentic Ito Jackuchu (1716–1800), *byobu* shelters the gathering from the chill northerly breezes that have only just begun to blow.

The small party is a privileged one. The hosts set a lighted *hibachi* brazier in front of each guest. The visitors help themselves to tobacco from drawers in the *hibachi*, fill ornate bamboo chillums, light up and release dense puffs of fog. Strands of smoke coil up like a thick nebulous rope as they leave through a hole in the ceiling.

Refreshments are served from a *mizuya* rolled in from the kitchen. Paper screens are drawn open and shut, revealing a *kaidan* stepped-*tansu* leading up into an attic. Other cabinets may also have been observed. Made of zelkova, paulownia, cryptomeria and cypress, some of them feature ornate motifs, including the *daimyo* crests of forebears.

The conversation is initially desultory but grows animated with the passage of time and as *sake* flows from jars preserved in another *tansu*. Topics slide from taxes and the rising prices of rice, to politics, pestilence and calamities – wars, arson, earthquakes, the furies of Fuji-san, the forging of hot springs as a consequence of local geological tumult, and, of course, the fire of 1657.

The scene above, a tapestry of fictional provenance, could well represent a slice from the history of home and hospitality in traditional Japan. The interior is appointed with objects derived from strictly historical sources and one might truly have found a teahouse such as this in post-1657 Edo.

Opposing Metaphors

Wood and fire are mutually opposed metaphors in the Japanese psyche. Frequent earthquakes, on the one hand, made it hard to build homes with heavier materials such as stone and brick. On the other, the use of fire, essential for cooking and heating living quarters in cold winters, made wooden homes vulnerable. The infernal blaze of 1657 that raged three entire days and left 107,000 people dead and thousands homeless is etched deep in the minds of the Japanese.

The fire broke out on 2 March in the temple of Honmyo-ji. The air was dry after months of winter drought and flames were quick to spread. The streets of Edo were very narrow, with gates and barriers built everywhere to make it difficult for potential insurgents to congregate.

According to Zacharias Waganaer, head of a Dutch East India trade mission visiting Edo at the time, the fire was a, "rolling sea of flame [that was] a mile wide running from east to west and it pressed forward with fire sparks falling like a strong rain…"

Right: Exposed to the elements, the stone-cobbled inner courtyard of a traditional Japanese home. Here, by convention, footwear is removed before stepping into the *tatami* matted interior of the home.

The event highlights the role of the *nagamochi kuruma*, a rather heavy chest on wheels usually kept in a separate storehouse built of fireproof earth. Unlike the light pieces of functional furniture that stand unobtrusively in remote corners of a living room or hidden behind paper screens – that chest on wheels took centre stage in the tragedy. In fleeing the scene of the fire, people loaded their *nagamochi kuruma* and attempted to force their way through the clogged lanes of the town, serving only to add further clutter. Many people died clinging to their chattels, from heavy burns or through suffocation. One of the first items to be placed on the banned list following the fire was the big chest with four wheels.

The source of the 1657 fire was the temple. It could as well have been an *irori* or *hibachi* or wicker lamp lit before household deities. Also, the fireproof earthen silos – in which only the wealthy could afford to keep their *tansus* – proved to be not so fireproof.

On the flip side, the early Edo event is important for the history of Japanese traditional furniture. Historians agree that the term *tansu* is primarily applicable to cabinetry created during the post-fire Edo period (1657–1868), which became a time of frenetic rebuilding and innovation.

Understated Elegance

Tansu is no "fine art" and cannot be categorised as classical. Collectors and connoisseurs across the world are willing to pay significant prices for them because of their simple and well-preserved elegance, as well as the fact that before the Meiji restoration of 1869 every article of *tansu* was made uniquely to address a specific need of the customer.

The ordinary Japanese had no decorative furniture as in the western world. They sat on cushions on *tatami* mats; they ate at low tables that permitted little creative interpretation; and, they slept on *futons* on elevated *tatami* platforms. The only scope for furniture was for storing personal effects like clothing, writing materials, implements and documents. These appeared on the scene only with the rise of the merchant as a class and the ensuing differentiation and complexity that became evident in the society.

The one predominant design ethic of the *tansu* all through its 200-year history is the primacy of function over form. For all its elegance and appeal, one must not forget that the *tansu* was quite literally a humble chest for chattels.

The Japanese word *tansu* is made up of two particles, Tan and Su, representing, in their bare social context, 'food silo' and the verb 'to carry bamboo or wood'. The first occurrence of the word is traced to records in the second half of the early Edo period referred to as the Genroku era (1688–1703).

The wood for the *tansu* came from the mountain forests of Japan. The case, exposed frame members, and drawers were made of cryptomeria and cypress – among the evergreens – and zelkova, chestnut, and paulownia – among the broad-leaved variety. Wood for marquetry, lining of compartments, panelling, decorative facing, and interior framing came from soft cuts of these woods or from occasionally imported mulberry, persimmon, and sandalwood.

The design element in *tansu* can be traced to the Zen perspective on life in Japan. Introduced from China in the 12th century, Zen emphasised the continuity between nature and human life, and advocated self-discipline, austerity of habits, and pursuit of self-knowledge.

The Zen penchant for conundrum rather than *problématique* readily found converts among the Japanese aristocracy. The emperor, the shogun military governors, the daimyo feudal barons, and the samurai professional warriors accepted the Zen ethic, encouraging frankness, loyalty and steadfastness.

The aesthetic of 7th and 8th century Japan was moulded by a royal decree in 646 to emulate political models based on Confucian legal codes. As a consequence, tribal kinship-based government made way for a more centralised rule with a bureaucracy.

The earliest examples of Japanese woodcraft are preserved in the *Shoso-in*, an imperial storehouse that stood in the grounds of a temple in Nara. Among them is a cabinet, called a *zushi*, made of zelkova wood burl with lacquer finish.

The Shinden Style

The Fujiwara rulers introduced the shinden style, modifying Chinese lines to suit the more spontaneous Japanese ethos. It did away with chairs and beds, and fixed walls that partitioned interior space. The living quarters would instead use sliding panels; a shallow-raised platform of two *tatami* mats in the middle of the room for sleeping *chodai*; a *tatami* mat six centimetres high placed on either side of the *chodai*; free-standing open-frame placed nearby *tana;* and folding screens enclosing the area where lay the *tatami* mats *byobu*.

Cabinetmakers for the aristocracy were able to develop a style that was uniquely Japanese and introduced the open frame shelves. For instance, the *nikai-zushi* was known for its double doors opening outward and its splayed legs while the *nikai-dana* featured a semi-enclosed frame of two shelves. The second retained the interconnected frame of the T'ang but the four splayed legs were of original imagination.

From the 10th century to the 17th century, Japan saw the emergence of the samurai and the tea ceremony as a social and sacred ritual. The samurai brought in a sense of the ephemeral – a warrior's life was like a water bubble, open and vulnerable.

The warm tones of wooden floor, low cabinet and pine beams welcome visitors at the entrance to a Kyoto home.

This growth of the Zen spirit saw the weakening of central authority and the emergence of feudal states. Feudal strength was dissipated in the pursuit of political ambition through warfare. Commerce was encouraged to enable the generation of wealth to pay for the war efforts.

About this time two technologies became available that related to cutting timber: the vertical saw operated by two men that could slice through timber of large girth, and the planer device that allowed slivers to be shaved off thin wood. These tools allowed the building of massive structures such as castles and big houses and, before long, moved from forestry to the cabinetmaker's workshop.

In 1575, General Oda Nobunaga (1510–1582) ended the political ambitions of religious and sectarian denominations. The peace that ensued allowed merchants to prosper: the demand for cabinets rose and *tansu* began to evolve.

Multi-level freestanding shelves developed into merchandise drawers or *shohin hikidashi*, the direct predecessors of the *tansu*. The scissors box *hasami bako* innovation, in the shape of clamps for insertion of bamboo poles or hemp ropes, made it easier to carry. Peddlers and tradesmen of the middle and later Edo period would carry their wares and tools in these scissors boxes. The *hasami-bako* lugged by the tinsmith of later days was a curious innovation. Of two compartments, one was rigged out with a bellows for kindling and sustaining fires for tin working.

Nobunaga's successor, Toyotomi Hideyoshi (1536–1598), decreed that rice fields were the primary source of tax revenue for the government. He allowed only the samurai, drafted for policing and revenue gathering, to carry swords and banned foreign trade. After Hideyoshi, Tokugawa Ieyasu (1542–1616), chose the fishing village of Edo on the Kanto plains east of Kyoto, as the site of his new capital.

The merchant, hitherto considered unproductive, had to work his way up and through the hierarchy to gain in wealth and status. In the process, he became instrumental in the comprehensive development of the lower classes, the spread of commerce, and the support of secondary trades.

The Samurai Home

The samurai had *sho-dansu* made for books pertaining to music, poetry, religion, and literature and kept their swords in the *katana-dansu*. They used the *goyo-nagamochi* to store clothing and official documents and *kosode-dansu* for short-sleeved silk kimonos. The samurai woman had the *temoto-dansu* for use in the privacy of her rooms. There was also the *isho-dansu*, a clothing chest containing multiple drawers to store seasonal costumes.

The tea ceremony chest *cha-dansu* was a portable cabinet containing bowls and other accompaniments of the tea making ritual. The materials employed to build the *cha-dansu* would vary according to the season of use, and whether it was to be placed outdoors or indoors.

Landowners and government functionaries among the farmers used two types of cabinets. The infamous *nagamochi kuruma* continued to be used outside Edo, Kyoto and Osaka. The *mizuya* chest-on-chest cabinetry was a frame-and-panel work of shelves and sliding doors used for storing cooking utensils and kept in the vicinity of the kitchen. *Mizuya* was commonly associated with the area used in preparing for the tea ceremony.

After the Genroku era (1688–1703), merchants prospered and gained control over the logistics of supply and distribution. Merchant *tansu* stored merchandise, commercial documents and articles of personal use. Merchandise cabinets, *shohin hikidashi*, were used in shops since the early Edo. The *kusuri-dansu* were lightweight medicine chests meant for backpacking. The *kaidan-dansu* or staircase-chest doubled as storage and as structural element in the shop.

Gyosho-bako was the peddler's mobile storage container. It was light and had compartments for storage of goods for sale or implements of trade. In the lesser towns, peddlers sold articles of daily use that included groceries and perishables such as vegetables, milk, fish, and eggs. Trinkets and items of luxury purchased in bigger towns such as Kyoto were also dispensed, together with big town dreams and gossip.

In the urban areas, cabinetry associated with shop administration was called *cho-dansu*. These elegant cabinets were made of hard woods and lined with hardware for both style and security.

The *choba-goshi* was a two or three-sided, configurable screen, with hinges separating each side, that offered privacy around the accountant's desk. The *choba-zukue* was the writing desk; the *kakesuzuri*, a box for important writing utensils; while the *in-bako* held less important shop seals. The more crucial piece of shop furniture was the *masutsuki zeni-bako* or the money box. This featured a coin slot that was usable by the sales employees when the master was away.

A secret compartment in the *cho-dansu* was used to keep debt instruments and pledge agreements.

Keeping the Merchants in their Place

The emergence of the merchant class as an economic force touched a sore nerve among the elite. The disparity between the two classes widened so rapidly that the shoguns found it necessary to invent means to prevent the merchant class from using symbols of wealth that would have made the chasm evident. It resorted to some ridiculous measures.

Through the Kansei Reform of 1789 the shogun's regent Matsudaira Sadanobu (1758–1892) restricted the design of clothing chests used by the merchants. Only one mid 18th century style of double-door chest-on-chest of paulownia wood was allowed. As a result, shop interiors remained fossils of design and craftsmen couldn't give free rein to their creative imagination until the late Edo period.

Other restrictions included a moratorium on the profession of barbers and hairdressers, a ban on house repairs, a prohibition of the wearing of clothes not sanctioned by the dress code, a ban on gambling, and segregation of the sexes at public baths.

The dawn of the Meiji period in 1868 ended the restrictions but encouraged industrial mass production. The imminent extinction of traditional *tansu* was mitigated to an extent by the emergence of regional *tansu*.

Sendai contributed merchant *tansu* for use in the *dei*, a *tatami* room where guests were entertained. It is better known for the massive chest with somewhat heavy engraved and embossed hardware against a zelkova frame with lacquer finish. Representative of the Iwayado *tansu* of Iwate prefecture was also a massive chest on wheels with multiple drawers for clothing fastened with vertical locking bars.

The commercially powerful coastal town of Sakata in Yamagata boasted boldly designed lacquered chest-on-chest with square drawers set against back plates with a motif of four diamonds.

Sado Island was known for the creation of merchant and trousseau *tansu*. The hardware was reminiscent of another genre of sea chests used on sailing ships conveying mainly rice between Japanese ports. These were characterised by the use of zelkova burl for face wood and cut decoration in the hardware.

Peddlers' cabinets continued to appear on the narrow streets of Edo after the Meiji era ended in 1912. Chronicles of the late thirties refer to armies of peddlers marching among the narrow lanes of suburban Edo, dispensing life's necessities,

Shades of twilight suffuse the interior of a *tatami* matted living room.

from foodstuffs to hobby goods, from knickknacks to trinkets, from plant and flower seedlings to miniature aquariums.

But the romance of old-style peddling would soon come to an end. Already in the 30s Edo was growing gaunt, clumsy, and unwieldy – a colloid of the weird synergies of modern technology and animistic Shinto. Post-war restoration created a demand for furnishing that local factories and old style *tansu* passed on.

There has long been an interest in *tansu*. Originals fetch high prices at international auctions of antiques. But from a 'Western' collector's point of view authentic *tansu* are becoming increasingly hard to come by, owing to the fact that their numbers were small to begin with.

The underside of the growing demand for bona fide *tansu* is the emergence of the ersatz. Gratefully, however, a number of scholarly works on the wood and techniques of *tansu* have come to the aid of the serious collector seeking to distinguish the real from the dubious.

筆筒

HONSHU PREFECTURE

Located in western Japan, Honshu Prefecture lies near the centre of the Japanese archipelago. The Chugoku Mountains neatly divide the province into northern and southern halves. It is the only prefecture in central Honshu to enjoy coasts on the Sea of Japan in the north and the Pacific Ocean in the south. Due to its location near the historic capitals of Nara and Kyoto, the province has a protracted history of countless battles fought between warlords and the Shogunate in feudal times.

Stepped chest of keyaki, Japanese elm and cypress wood. This versatile cabinet afforded access to an upper floor and simultaneously provided welcome storage space. Kansai. Late 19th century.

A Kaidan *tansu*, stepped chest, was an engineer's solution for Japanese homes where space limitations restricted storage and precluded fixed stairways. Kyoto. Late 19th century.

 Stepped chest of cryptomeria wood with
exceptionally narrow treads, intended probably for
a shop interior. Kansai. Taisho Period (1912).

Right: A dual-purpose Kaidan *tansu*, stepped chest, provided both
access to upper floors and efficient storage space as seen here in the
home of the Kyoto artist Yasuhiko Kida. Kyoto. Late 19th century.

Elegantly proportioned lacquer cabinet with open shelves for the storage of tea ceremony paraphernalia. Kyoto. Circa 1900.

Lacquer stand for sheet music. *Sugi*, or cryptomeria wood, considered one of Japan's most important forest trees. Kyoto. Early 20th century.

Mizuya, kitchen cabinet, with narrow upper sliding doors and lower recessed sliding doors with open display shelf of Negoro lacquer. Shiga Prefecture. Late 19th century.

Merchant's accounts chest of keyaki burl wood, displaying its distinctive grain. Shopkeepers commonly used chests of this type to store receipts and documents – and most importantly, the merchant's official seal. Kansai. Late 19th century.

Isho *tansu*, clothing storage chest in three sections, to be either stacked or used individually. Made of keyaki burl wood – cherished for its distinctive grain. Kansai. Late 19th century.

HYOGO PREFECTURE

Hyogo Prefecture is situated at the geographical centre of Japan. Kobe, which experienced a severe earthquake in the 1990s, is the prefecture's capital city. Hyogo has served as the country's gateway since feudal times, facilitating cultural exchanges between Japan and the West.

Left: Crowded shop interior of a dealer specialising in *tansu* and scholars items.

Merchant's accounts chest. Keyaki wood with excellent metal work. Of special note are the interesting floral design hinges. Kansai. Late 19th century.

Isho *tansu*, clothing storage chest. Front panels are of keyaki wood. The elaborate metal fittings are typical of the Sendai region, one of the few furniture making centres in Japan that resumed production after World War II. Late 19th century.

Chest of drawers. Front panels are of keyaki wood with *Sugi,* cryptomeria wood used for the casing. The scroll form half lock plates are typical of chests from the Sendai region of Northeastern Honshu. 19th century.

 Ryobiraki isho *tansu*, storage chest of Paulownia wood with pronounced metal work. Upper cabinet has a two-door compartment with two drawers and a lockable compartment in the lower section. Lock plates fitted with a double-action mechanism were a late 19th century innovation. Yamagata Prefecture. Early 20th century.

 Merchant's accounts chest of *Sugi*, cryptomeria wood, with sliding doors and a lockable compartment. Compact in size, it rested either directly on *tatami* matting or was placed on a work shelf for easy access. Yamagata Prefecture. Early 20th century.

 Merchant's accounts chest. The front façade is of cypress wood, the casing of *Sugi*, cryptomeria wood. Precious woods were favoured for front panels since *tansu* were often fitted into niches where only the front would be visible. Meiji Period (late 1800s).

Left: Detail of metal work applied to a keyaki wood Choba *tansu* chest. Cabinets enhanced by elaborate metal fittings were more popular than cupboards embellished with simple lock plates and hinges.

Choba *tansu*, a merchant's accounts chest, used for the storage of documents and company seals and were prominently displayed to impress the merchant's clients. Made of keyaki, Japanese elm wood. Taisho Period, 1912.

 Choba *tansu*, document chest of orange-red Negoro-nuri lacquer. Shiga Prefecture. Late 19th century.

 Storage chest in red lacquer. These chests are unique to the area around Lake Biwa, east of Kyoto. Negoro lacquer with its fine patina, was perfected by monks from the temple complex of Wakayama in the 13th century.

 Isho *tansu*, clothing chest, in Negoro-nuri red lacquer. Furniture showing wear from use, such as revealing the undercoating of black lacquer is particularly esteemed. Early 20th century.

ASIAN
FURNITURE
JAPAN
289

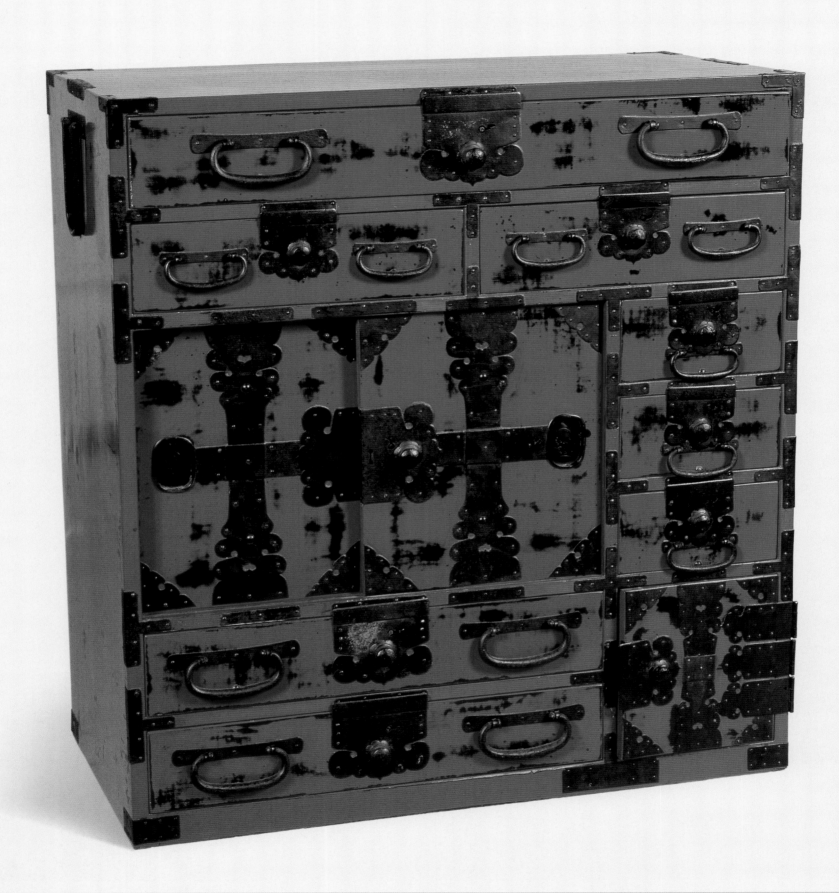

ASIAN
FURNITURE
JAPAN
290

Choba *tansu*, document chest, of
Negoro-nuri lacquer with elaborate
hand-forged metal fittings. Ishikawa
Prefecture. 19th century.

Right: Negoro-nuri (lacquerware). Wakayama Prefecture is regarded as one of Japan's
three major centres of lacquer production. Lacquerware has been produced here since
the Muromachi era, when monks from the Negoro-dera Temple near Kihoku first created
beautifully lacquered pots and trays for their everyday use.

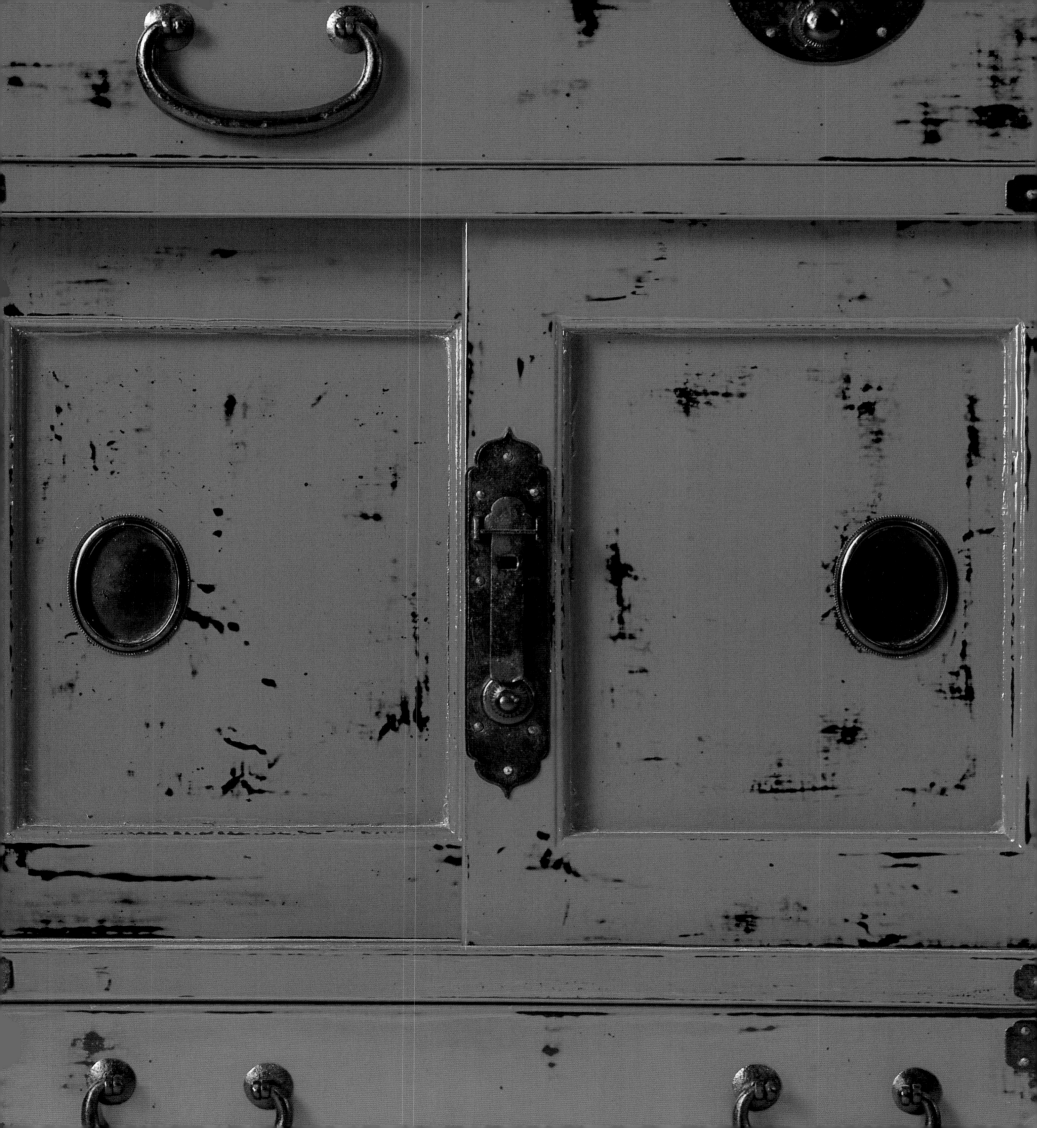

Four-drawer, isho *tansu*, cabinet, of Negoro-nuri red lacquer. The cabinet, of light Japanese elm wood, consists of two sections stacked one upon the other, though the sections can also be used as individual pieces of furniture. Shiga Prefecture. Contemporary.

Scholar's writing box of keyaki burr (Japanese elm wood), to store calligraphy brushes, inkstones, water droppers, seals and objects associated with the scholar. Kansai Prefecture. Early to mid 18th century. (left) The same cabinet with doors opened to reveal the inside.

Cho-bako *funa-dansu* (ship chest). Opened doors reveal five drawers of varying sizes, made of keyaki burr (Japanese elm wood), with Kiri and Paulownia interiors. Strap iron is affixed to the casing. The chest also has (though hidden by the opened doors) handles and rings to facilitate being carried on a shoulder pole. Kansai Prefecture. Late Edo, early Meiji Period.

 Kuruma tansu, wheeled chest. The wheels concealed by the deep lower apron. Ring pulls enable the *tansu* to be quickly rolled to safety in times of emergency. Yamagata Prefecture. Early 19th century.

 Wheeled chest of keyaki, Japanese elm wood. Both upper and lower sections are fitted with two sliding doors each with horizontally recessed door panels. Metal braces are affixed to four corners and central mainstay with metal handles and wheel ring pulls on both sides. Supported on wheels, these *tansu* could be rolled to safety during times of emergency. Iwate Prefecture. Early 19th century.

Eight-drawer Sendai isho *tansu* wedding chest.
Keyaki wood drawer fronts and sugi (oedai) casing.
Sendai-type front lock plates of iron. Ornately
adorned with metal fittings. 19th century.

Six-drawer wedding chest from Sendai. The
front façade is of keyaki wood and the case
of cypress. Heavily adorned with Meiji-era
iron fittings. 19th century.

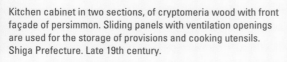

Kitchen cabinet in two sections, of cryptomeria wood with front façade of persimmon. Sliding panels with ventilation openings are used for the storage of provisions and cooking utensils. Shiga Prefecture. Late 19th century.

Two curio display cabinets with open shelves and doors decorated with mother-of-pearl inlay. Both cabinets display elements of Western influences with the incorporation of protruding curvilinear aprons. Meiji Period, 1800s.

Futon tansu used to store bedding during the day. Made of mixed woods. Kansai Prefecture. Late 19th century.

Right: Storage cabinet with front façade of keyaki veneer. Designed strictly for utility with sliding door compartments, inner shelves and numerous small drawers. Like staircase *tansu*, kitchen cabinets display a minimum of ironwork and rarely have locking drawers or doors. Shiga Prefecture. Late Edo Period.

The ornately decorated front portal of the Sutra
Library, Rinno-ji Temple, Nikko, built during
Japan's self-imposed era of seclusion during
which the country's arts and economy flourished.
Edo Period 1600–1867.

Camphor (*tanxiang*). Because of its resistance to insects and its attractive grain, camphor wood has long been used for making wardrobes and storage chests. It's not uncommon to see camphor trees rise to a height of 50 metres with a diameter of 5 metres. When freshly cut, the fragrance is intense and does not diminish with time. It is soft to medium in hardness, relatively stable and can be polished to a rich lustre.

Northern Elm (*Yumu*) is the most common furniture-making wood found throughout northern China. Like Japanese Elm (chunyu), it reaches an average height of 30 metres and a metre in diameter. It is of medium density and hardness, resistant to decay and easy to work. The grain reveals feather-like features – popular in furniture making.

Locust (*Huai*) is categorised as a 'miscellaneous hardwood', posing sawing difficulties similar to those of Northern Elm; however the wood is appreciably denser and the surface more coarsely textured. The grain is relatively straight. It is an easy wood to dry and suffers little warping. It is resistant to moisture and insect damage and when worked, reveals a lustrous surface.

Zelkova (Keyaki), are deciduous trees, of which four of the five known species are natives of Asia. Zelkovas are handsome trees that provide wonderful shade. Japanese Zelkova (Keyaki) is a slow-growing tree that may reach the height of 20 metres with either single or multiple trunks. The smooth wood is dense and hard, pliable and heavy, and is used predominantly for the manufacture of furniture.

Cypress (*Bimu*). Late Ming connoisseurs noted the use of Sichuan Cypress as a greatly desired furniture-making material. The Weeping Cypress is the most highly regarded for its timber. It has brown tonality and is sometimes streaked with red. With prolonged exposure to air and light, the tones become richer. The wood has an attractive lustre, is oily to the touch and has a strong fragrance.

Paulownia (*Wutong, Baotong*). Because of its sound resonant qualities, the wood was favoured for centuries for the making of musical instruments in Japan. It has a low level of thermal conductivity and is thus employed for window frames and doors. With its high combustion point, it is sometimes considered a quasi-fireproof wood and is employed for the construction of *tansu* and coffers to store valuables.

Oak (*Zuomu, Gaoli mu*). Furniture made of oak is rare, though it has long been a favoured wood for elite pieces. Botanists have identified 140 varieties of oak widely distributed throughout Asia, inclusive of both deciduous and evergreen varieties. The heartwood is not clearly distinguished and ranges from grey-yellow to grey-brown with occasional streaks.

Huanghuali (*Huali*). The Chinese term *Huanghuali* literally means 'yellow flowering pear' wood, and identifies a member of the rosewood family. The modifier *huang* (yellowish-brown) was added in the early twentieth century to describe old *huali* wood whose surfaces had mellowed to a yellowish tone due to extended exposure to light. The finest *huanghuali* has a translucent shimmering surface with abstractly figured patterns that delight the eye. The colour can range from reddish-brown to golden-yellow.

Walnut (*Hetao*). Many examples of walnut furniture from the Shanxi region demonstrate refined workmanship. The surface of walnut tends to have more of an open-grained texture. The freshly worked wood emits a distinctive fragrance. Because its trees are generally cultivated for its fruit, Manchurian Walnut is often used in its place.

Nanmu Burl (*Douban Nan*) is frequently mentioned as a material par excellence in Ming recordings. It is often used for cabinet making, bookshelves, table top panels and small scholar's objects. Nanmu is a large, slow-growing tree of the evergreen family that develops into a tall, straight trunk achieving the height of 40 metres. It has a dense structured grain and ranges in tones from olive-brown to red-brown.

Boxwood (*Huangyang*) is a small tree, almost a shrub. It is rarely used for full-sized furniture and more often for small, carved objects or as decorative inlay. It is a durable wood, dense, fine and even textured, making it especially suitable for carving. The grain is straight and the wood does not dry easily. Freshly worked boxwood has an earthy fragrance. The surface polishes to a silky lustre.

Narra. The wood is derived from a relatively short-stemmed deciduous tree. It can reach a height of 30 metres with a trunk diameter of up to 7 metres. Narra is a durable hardwood with favourable processing abilities. The heartwood has a yellow-rose to brown colour with an ornamental texture that is decorative. It darkens upon exposure to light. If well dried, it hardly shrinks, is not prone to cracking and is resistant to fungi and insects.

CHINESE ROUND MALLET
For assembly work in cabinet making and carpentry. The mallet consists of red oak (Akagashi) head with a waxed oak handle.

CARPENTER'S MALLET
The trapezoidal head is made of extremely hard and dense laurel wood to guarantee maximal striking power. The handle is made of Shorea Robusta.

SPLITTING MAUL
Handy axe for splitting small to medium size firewood The head has a hardened poll designed for driving a splitting edge.

JAPANESE CURVED ADZE
One-handed adze for hollowing out bowls, seat bottoms, boats and for sculpturing.

EUROPEAN ADZE
19th century European Cooper's adze – a tool with curved blade used for shaping wood.

LATTHAMMER
Hammer heads were commonly cast of forged steel, tempered at both faces to provide the head with strength, resilience and balance.

COOPER'S BROAD AXE
18th century axe used for hewing and smoothing beams. Single bevelled blade, with a tapered, angled socket.

JAPANESE SPLITTING KNIFE
For splitting out wooden shingles, instrument ribs, boards etc. Splitting knives should only be struck with a wooden mallet.

CHINESE FRAME (BOW) SAW
Frame saws have been in use since ancient times. A wooden frame with tensioning stick and toggle bar holds the saw blade taut. Used in the cutting of curved woodwork.

CHINESE HARDWOOD BACKSAW
Rustic saw with crude wooden handle used primarily in agriculture (pruning of trees) as opposed to actual carpentry.

VENEER SAW
During the Japanese Edo Period, the refined skill of sawing diversified into a number of narrow specialities. Saws came in many varieties conceived for specific uses.

DUAL-HANDED FILE
Reproduced from 13th century original. Dual-handed files (rasps) were employed by two people, one at each end to plane and make smooth wood surfaces.

DOZUKI MINI
For cutting dowels, pegs, tenons etc. flush to the surface of the wood without damaging its surface. Flexible blades with teeth of limited cutting depth.

MORTISE CHISEL
Heavy-duty chisel especially designed for making rectangular mortises. The blades are laminated with white paper steel.

DOVETAIL CHISEL (OIRE NOMI TAKEI)
Elegant light-duty chisel for finishing dovetails and other joinery. Thin, laminated blades with finely tapered sides.

JAPANESE HAND-FORGED CHISEL
Chisels from the discipline of Shogun sword-makers are one item among the carpenter's many tools that require precision and clear-cut edges.

TSAI BENCH CHISEL
Mainly used by temple carpenters, Tsai chisels appeal to woodworkers with deep appreciation of fine tools.

SHOVEL GOUGE
Spade-shaped blades with oak handles. For two-handed use. Ideal for deep hollowing, like the making of masks, drums and other large scale carving projects.

FISH HEAD (KOBIKI) SAW
Capable of cutting on upper and lower edge. Blades are extremely thin with teeth less than 1mm apart. Beautifully proportioned, perfectly balanced and a pleasure to use.

CROWN MINI CHISEL
This compact chisel provides maximum cutting control, by allowing the carpenter to get close to the workpiece. Ideal for cleaning up fittings and wood joints.

FRENCH BEVEL-GEAR DRILL
19th century French carpenter's bevel-gear drill with changeable bits. Head and handle made of wood.

ENGLISH BOXWOOD DRILL
19th century English boxwood bow drill with brass fittings and steel chick for gripping the bit. Cuts equally in both directions. Used for light wood, metal or stone work.

JAPANESE INKPOT
The bowl contained fine black (or white) powder and was employed for describing long straight lines that needed to be sawn.

CHINESE INKPOT
Chinese inkpots of blackwood have in modern times been replaced by chalk-line reels. The bowl contained fine powder through which a thread was passed, held taut, then snapped to create a straight fine line.

ENGLISH *JARVIS* PLANE
19th century European wheel rights *Jarvis* plane, used for the rounding of wheel spokes, barrels, dowels or rungs.

ALPINE PLANE
19th century Alpine smoothing plane with integral handles and added front grip with which to push and pull the plane.

CHINESE PLANE (MU BAO)
The design of Chinese planes is similar to the Japanese Kanna. The difference being that the Chinese plane can be employed on the pull or the push stroke, whereas the Japanese plane can only be used on the pull stroke.

MINI BENCH PLANE
Elegantly carved Ebony (Hei Tan) body. Blade angle at 60 degrees and wooden wedge. The wooden blocks are the most captivating feature of a Chinese plane.

COOPER'S CROZE
18th century triple screw stemmed Cooper's croze with a decorative shell carving to the stock. Used for cutting grooves into barrels.

COOPER'S CROZE
19th century European triple screw stemmed plane with handles on either side to facilitate pushing or pulling the plane.

EUROPEAN GROOVING PLANE
19th century Austrian or Bavarian adjustable, triple wood screw grooving plane, with adjustable fence. Used for cutting precise grooves e.g. for making of sliding doors.

SCOTTISH CRAFTSMAN PLANE
19th century Scottish made handle beech plough plane. Various brass fittings including thumb-screw and locking device are located on the side.

CEREMONIAL TOOL BOX
Tool boxes were trophies to aspire to at the end of an arduous apprenticeship. They were honourably presented to the craftsman at temple festivals by a priest or local dignitary.

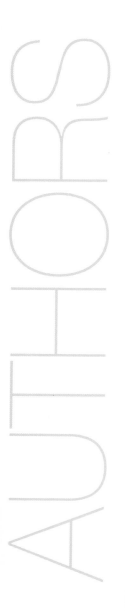

INDIA

Peter Moss was born in India, where he spent his childhood. His experience of Asia has encompassed the transition from colonialism to independence in both India (1947) and Malaya (1957), the birth of Malaysia in 1963 and the return of Hong Kong to China in 1997. From 1978 to his retirement from Hong Kong's civil service in 1993 he was Assistant Director in charge of publicity in the Government Information Services, producing books on the history, heritage and mapping of Hong Kong. His twenty-one published works since then include books on Asian history, arts, culture and symbolism, together with five novels.

INDONESIA

Soedarmadji Damais is an independent scholar and curator specialising in the art and culture of Indonesia. He has studied the architecture, languages, literature and history of Indonesia both within Indonesia and in France. Between 1971 and 1974 he was the historical and cultural advisor to the Old Jakarta Kota Restoration Office, involved in the conception and design of several Jakarta museums, among them the Jakarta History Museum (1974), the Jakarta Art Gallery (1976), the Jakarta Textile Museum and the Jakarta Maritime Museum (1977). In 1989 he was appointed director of the Jakarta History Museum. He currently serves on the Board of officers of the Indonesian Body for Artistic Cooperation (Badan Kerjasama Kesenian Indonesia) and is chairman of the Bharata Foundation for Javanese "Wayang Wong" theatre (Yayasan Bharata).

THAILAND

Pitya Bunnag was educated in England and graduated from the London School of Industrial and Product Design. He returned to Thailand to work with the Thai Design Centre under the auspices of the Ministry of Industrial Promotion. From 1995–1999 he held the post of Honorary Editor of the Journal of the Siam Society. He is presently lecturer at the Department of Fine Arts at Chiang Mai University, Thailand. His publications include: *The First Muslim Leader of Siam*, by Silpawattanatham Publications, Bangkok 2005. *Sema Sima: The Monastic Boundary Stone Markers of the Ayutthaya Period* by the Thailand Research Fund, Bangkok.

CHINA

Willy Wo-lap Lam has been researching and writing about China for more than thirty years, and is a recognised authority on areas including the Chinese Communist Party, public administration, foreign policy, the People's Liberation Army, as well as the country's economic and political reform. Dr Lam has worked in senior editorial positions in international media including *Asiaweek*, *South China Morning Post*, and the Asia-Pacific Headquarters of CNN. He was an accredited Beijing-based foreign correspondent from 1986 to 1989. In 2004 he was appointed Professor of China & Global Studies at Akita International University, an English-speaking, public university in Japan. He has published six books on China, including *The Era of Jiang Zemin* (Prentice Hall/Pearson, 1999); *China after Deng Xiaoping* (John Wiley & Sons, 1995); and *Chinese Politics in the Hu Jintao Era* (M E Sharpe, 2006). His books have been translated into Chinese and Japanese.

TIBET

Anna Hestler is a freelance writer with a keen interest in Asian cultures. She has written for several Asian publishers. Born in Canada, Anna studied at the School of Oriental and African Studies in the United Kingdom. After graduating, she spent a year in Indonesia and then moved to Hong Kong, where she lived for almost a decade. She worked at Oxford University Press China before deciding to pursue full-time writing. She now lives in New York City.

PHILIPPINES

Martin I Tinio Jr, a businessman and gentleman farmer, is also an antiques collector, world traveller, genealogist, historian and gourmet. Educated in Europe and the United States, he is a former museum curator and writes on Philippine cooking and social history, as well as on architecture, furniture, silver, jewellery and ivory of the Spanish-Philippine colonial period.

KOREA

Anthony Banks has lived in both Japan and Korea since 1992, working at Seoul National University in Korea amongst other institutions. He has studied East Asian history at The School of Oriental & African Studies, University of London, as well as at the University of Tsukuba, Japan. He has gathered material in the form of photographs and personal interviews on the traditional wood crafts of Korea (as well as a personal research collection) with the aim of producing a definitive guidebook for those interested in this furniture tradition. Anthony is currently working as a teacher trainer at the Sungkyungwan-Georgetown TESOL program in Seoul, Korea.

JAPAN

Yokobori Yoichi is a journalist, writer, and Professor of International Affairs, Politics and Culture at Wayo Womans University, Tokyo. Born in Sheng Yang, North China, he spent his youth in Taiwan before World War II and then returned to Japan. He studied at the International Christian University (ICU-Tokyo), Harvard University in 1960, and the International Peace Academy in Helsinki in 1971. He is a senior writer, editor and translator for Kyodo News Agency.

India

Pages 9, 11, 13, 15, 17 – FormAsia Books, Hong Kong

Pages 21, 28, 29, 30, 31, 32, 34, 35, 42 – 43 – The Taj Mahal Hotel, Mumbai, India

Pages 22, 23, 24(l), 25(b), 33, 36, 37, 38, 39, 40, 41 – The Victoria and Albert Museum, London

Pages 24(r), 25(t), 26, 27 – Ravissant, Mumbai, India

Coordinators and logistics: Manmeet Sidu, The Taj Mahal Hotel, Mumbai; Deepa Nand, Mumbai

Indonesia

Pages 45, 47, 55 – FormAsia Books, Hong Kong

Pages 48, 72(c), 73(b-l), 76(l & r-b), 77(t & b-l) – Foundation for the Indonesia Archives Building, Jakarta. Curator: Tamalia Alisjahbana LLB

Pages 49, 66 – Laya Suharnoko

Pages 51, 67, 73(t-l) – Lana Sumendap Saliot

Page 53 – Café Batavia, Jakarta.

Pages 57, 69 – Ghea Penggabean

Pages 58(l-t & r), 59, 61 – Wieneke de Groot

Pages 58(l-b), 64(l-t & l-b), 65(t-l & t-r), 71, 75(b), 79(t) – Family Suharnoko

Pages 60, 80 – 81 – Iwan Terta

Pages 62, 63, 64(r), 65(b), 70, 72(l & r), 73(t-r & b-r), 75(t), 76(r-t), 77(b-r), 79(b) – Museum Sejarah, Jakarta. Curator: Dra Tinia Budiati MA

Page 68 – Bagoes S. Brotodiwirjo

Page 74 – Mrs Margaret Alisjahbana

Page 78 – Losari Coffee Plantation, Magelang, Indonesia

Coordinators and logistics: Lani Sirnarwi, Jakarta; Poomeswari N., Hong Kong

Thailand

Pages 83, 85 – FormAsia Books, Hong Kong

Pages 87, 89, 104, 105, 114 – 115 – The James H.W. Thompson Foundation, Bangkok

Pages 93, 100, 102, 107, 108(t), 110, 111 – The Prasart Museum, Bangkok

Pages 95(l), 97(l), 98, 101(l & r-b) – The National Museum of Thailand, Bangkok

Page 95(r) – Garuda: Rare Objects, Bangkok

Pages 96, 103, 108(b) – The Suan Pakkard Palace Museum, Bangkok

Page 97(r) – Pailin Gallery, Bangkok

Pages 99(l), 112-113 – Asia Art Antique, Bangkok

Pages 99(r), 101(r-t) – Chart Antique, Bangkok

Page 106 – Marisa Viravaidya

Page 109 – Darapirom Museum, Chulalongkorn University, Chiang Mai

Coordinators and logistics: Marisa Viravaidya, Bangkok; Cludine Nicole Triolo; Dhara Devi, Chiang Mai

China

Pages 117, 119, 144(t-r), 157(b-r) – FormAsia Books, Hong Kong

Page 121 – The China Club, Hong Kong

Page 123 – The Luk Yu Teahouse, Hong Kong

Page 124 – The University of Hong Kong

Pages 127(l), 130(r-b), 132, 135(r-t), 139(l-b), 140, 141(r), 144(t-l), 145(t-r), 159 – Zitan Oriental Antiques, Hong Kong

Pages 127(r), 133(r-b), 138 (r-b), 145(b), 147(l-t), 154(r-t & r-b), 155, 156(l), 157(t-l & t-r) – Altfield Gallery, Hong Kong

Pages 128(l), 151(r-t & r-b), 154(l), 156(r), 157(b-l) – Honeychurch Antiques, Hong Kong

Pages 128(r), 129 – Hanlin Gallery, Hong Kong

Pages 130(l), 131(l), 135(r-b), 144(b) – Ashwood Gallery, Thailand

Pages 130(r-t), 134, 137(r), 138(l), 141(l-b), 146, 147(l-b), 151(l) – China Art, Hong Kong

Pages 131(r-t & r-b), 139(r), 142, 143(b), 152, 153, 158 – Gangolf Geis Collection, Christie's, New York

Pages 133(l), 141(l-t) – The Red Cabinet, Hong Kong

Pages 133(r-t), 135(l), 137, 145(t-l) – Chine Gallery, Hong Kong

Pages 136(l), 138(r-t), 139(l-t), 143(t), 148, 160 – Hobbs & Bishops Fine Arts, Hong Kong

Pages 147(r), 149, 150 – Andy Hei Ltd, Hong Kong

Page 161 – Lana Sumendap Saliot, Indonesia

Tibet

Pages 163, 165, 167, 169, 172 – FormAsia Books, Hong Kong

Pages 175, 176(r), 178, 179, 180(b-l & b-r), 181(t-r & b), 184(t, b-r & b-l), 187(t), 190, 191(b), 192, 193, 194(c) – Acala Gallery, Thailand

Pages 176(l), 177, 180(t), 181(t-l), 182, 183, 185, 186(l-t & l-b), 187(b), 188-189, 191(t), 194(l & r), 195 – Tibet House, Thailand

Pages 180(t), 184(t) – Theresa Coleman Fine Arts, Hong Kong

Page 186(r) – Chu's Tibetan Antiques, Hong Kong

Philippines

Pages 197, 199 – FormAsia Books, Hong Kong

Pages 200, 213(t-l), 216, 227 – Villa Escudero Plantation & Resort, Philippines

Pages 201, 203, 205, 209, 211, 212(l-t & l-b), 213(t-r & b), 215, 217, 218, 219, 220, 231 – Museo De La Salle, La Salle University, Philippines. Executive Directors: Ricardo Panlilio, Jose Ma

Pages 212(r), 228, 229 – Casa Manila, Philippines. Intramuros Administration. Acting Curator: Amelita Guillermo. Administrator: Dominador Ferrer, Jr. Sandra Martinez-Ching

Pages 214, 221(t-r) – Jamie C. Laya

Pages 221(b), 222, 225 – Luis Antonio & Cecile Gutierrez

Pages 221(t-l), 223(r), 224, 226, 230(l) – Paulino & Hetty Que

Coordinator and logistics: Olivia Lucas, Manila.

Korea

Pages 233, 235 – Corbis

Pages 239, 241, 243 – FormAsia Books, Hong Kong

Pages 245, 246, 247(t), 250(b-l & b-r), 252(r), 253, 254, 255, 259 – Seoul Furniture and Antique Co., Republic of Korea

Pages 247(b), 248, 249, 250(t), 251, 252(l), 256, 260, 261, 262(l), 264, 265 – National Folk Museum of Korea

Pages 237, 257, 258 – Falter Collection, Mainz, Germany

Coordinators and logistics: Tony Mitchell; Sumi Kim – Euro-Asian Heritage Development Ltd, Republic of Korea

Japan

Pages 267, 269, 300-301 – FormAsia Books, Hong Kong

Pages 271, 273, 279, 281, 282, 283(l & r-t), 286, 287, 290, 292, 293(b), 295, 296, 298, 299 – Maria Shobo, Kyoto, Japan

Page 275 – The Westin Miyako, Kyoto, Japan

Pages 277(l), 278(l), 280(l-t & l-b), 283(r-b), 284(r), 285, 288, 289, 291, 294(t) – Kenichi Kiyama, Otsu, Japan

Pages 277(r), 280(r), 293(t-l & t-r) – Honeychurch Antiques, Hong Kong

Pages 284(l), 294(b) – Falter Collection, Mainz, Germany

Page 297 – The Taj Mahal Hotel, Mumbai, India

Coordinator and logistics: Misa Matsumoto, The Westin Miyako, Kyoto, Japan

ASIAN FURNITURE
307

Legends:

b: bottom	b-l: bottom left	l-t: left top
c: centre	b-r: bottom right	l-b: left bottom
l: left	t-l: top left	r-b: right bottom
r: right	t-r: top right	r-t: right top
t: top